Helion & Company Limited
26 Willow Road
Solihull
West Midlands
B91 1UE
England
Tel. 0121 705 3393
Fax 0121 711 4075
email: info@helion.co.uk
website: www.helion.co.uk

Designed & typeset by Farr out Publications, Wokingham, Berkshire
Cover design by Paul Hewitt, Battlefield Design (www.battlefield-design.co.uk)
Printed by Henry Ling Ltd., Dorchester, Dorset

ISBN 978-1-911512-48-6

British Library Cataloguing-in-Publication Data
A catalogue record for this book is available from the British Library

CONTENTS

Note: In order to simplify the use of this book, all names, locations and geographic designations are as provided in *The Times World Atlas*, or other traditionally accepted major sources of reference, as of the time of described events. Correspondingly, the term 'Congo' designates the area of the former Belgian colony of the Congo Free State, granted independence as the Democratic Republic of the Congo in June 1960 and in use until 1971 when the country was renamed Republic of Zaire, which, in turn, reverted to Democratic Republic of the Congo in 1997, and which remains in use today. As such, Congo is not to be mistaken for the former French colony of Middle Congo (Moyen Congo), officially named the Republic of the Congo on its independence in August 1960, also known as Congo-Brazzaville.

GLOSSARY

ABAKO	*Alliance des Ba-Kongo* or Alliance of the Bakongo
AIB	Allied Intelligence Bureau
AU	African Union
BA	*Base Aérea* or Air Base
BCP	*Batalhão de Caçadores Pára-quedistas* or Paratroop Battalion
CECI	*Comando Especial de Contra Infiltração* or Special Command for Counter-Infiltration
CFB	*Caminho de Ferro de Benguela* or Benguela Railroad
COFI	*Comando Operacional das Forçes de Intervenção* or Operational Command of the Intervention Forces
CONAKAT	*Confédération des Associations Tribales du Katanga* or Confederation of the Tribal Associations of Katanga
COP	*Comando Operacional* or Operational Command
DAC	*Destacamento Avançado de Combate* or Advanced Combat Detachment
DGS	*Direcção-Geral Segurança* or General Security Directorate
ELNA	*Exército de Libertação Nacional de Angola* or Army for the National Liberation of Angola
EMP	*Escuela Militar de Pára-quedistas* or Military School of Parachuists
EPLA	*Exército Popular de Libertação de Angola* or Popular Army for the Liberation of Angola
FAP	*Força Aérea Portuguesa* or Portuguese Air Force
FARP	*Forças Armadas Revolucionárias de Povo* or Revolutionary Armed Forces of the People
FNLA	*Frente Nacional de Libertção de Angola* or National Front for the Liberation of Angola
FRELIMO	*Frente de Libertação de Moçambique* or Front for the Liberation of Mozambique
IAEM	*Instituto de Altos Estudos Militares* or Institute for Higher Military Studies
LDG	*Launcha de Desembarque Grande* or Large Landing Craft
LDM	*Launcha de Desembarque Média* or Medium Landing Craft
LZ	Landing Zone
MEDEVAC	Medical Evacuation (Aviation)
MNC	*Mouvement National Congolais* Congolese National Movement
MPLA	*Movimento Popular de Libertação de Angola* or Popular Movement for the Liberation of Angola
NATO	North Atlantic Treaty Organization
OAS	Organisation of African States
OAU	Organisation of African Unity
PAIGC	*Partido Africano da Independência da Guiné e Cabo Verde* or African Party for the Independence of Guiné and Cape Verde
PIDE	*Polícia Internacional de Defesa do Estado* or International Police for Defence of the State
RAF	Royal Air Force
RAAF	Royal Australian Air Force
RAN	Royal Australian Navy
RCP	*Regimento de Caçadores Pára-quedistas* or Parachute Regiment
RPG	Rocket-Propelled Grenade
SAM	Surface-to-Air Missile
SIPA	Société Industrielle Pour l'Aéronautique
SRD	Services Reconnaissance Department, Australian Army
TAP	*Transportes Aéreos Portugueses* or Portuguese Air Transport
TLCA	*Transporte Ligeiro de Carga Aérea* or Air Cargo Light Transport
UDI	Rhodesian Unilateral Declaration of Independence
UN	United Nations
UNITA	*União Nacional para a Independência Total de Angola* or the National Union for the Total Independence of Angola
UPA	*Uniao das Populações de Angola* or Union of Angolan Peoples
UTCI	*Unidade Táctica de Contra Infiltração* or Tactical Counter-Infiltration Unit
ZIL	*Zona de Intervenção Leste* or Eastern Intervention Zone
ZIN	*Zona de Intervenção Norte* or Northern Intervention Zone
ZML	*Zona Militar Leste* or Eastern Military Zone

INTRODUCTION

Between 1961 and 1974, Portugal faced the extremely ambitious task of conducting three simultaneous counterinsurgency campaigns in Angola, Guiné, and Mozambique. It was at the time neither a wealthy nor a well-developed country. In fact, it was the least wealthy Western European nation by most standards of economic measure. Thus for Portugal in 1961 to have mobilized an armed force, transported it many thousands of miles to its African colonies, established a sophisticated logistic infrastructure to support it, equipped it with special weapons and matériel, and trained it for a very specialized type of warfare was a remarkable achievement. It is made even more noteworthy by the fact that these tasks were accomplished without any previous experience, doctrine, or demonstrated competence in the field of either power projection or counterinsurgency warfare, and thus without the benefit of any instructors who were competent in these specialties. To put this last statement in perspective, other than periodic pacification efforts, Portugal had not fired a shot in anger in Africa since World War One, when Germany invaded northern Mozambique and southern Angola.

The Portuguese defence establishment was quite familiar with the principles of counterinsurgency, was aware that its troops were not going to fight a classic conventional war, and understood that forces had to be modified and adapted to the job at hand. There was substantial concern throughout the armed forces in undertaking what would be a wholesale and radical change in force structure and training, as it would affect all aspects of traditional tactics, techniques, and procedures. It would very much disturb the status quo and thus professional career paths. Nevertheless, Portugal proceeded to adapt its forces to a new way of war and created a force uniquely tailored to fight in this new struggle. It changed its forces to fit the war rather than trying to fight a war with the wrong forces.

One of the most noteworthy of these developments was the use of special forces to hunt the insurgents. The *Pára-quedistas*, Paratroopers, or simply "Paras" were the very first such special force and as such were predictably controversial. The Air Force was new and not afraid to experiment with new concepts. Its organiser, Kaúlza de Arriaga, was an innovative thinker and saw the mating of Paras with the helicopter as an effective way to tackle the vast spaces in Portuguese Africa and pursue and destroy insurgents successfully. Hence, the Paras became part of the new Air Force. This proved a stroke of genius, as with the advent of the helicopter, its acquisition in numbers by Portugal, and its combination with the Paras, air mobility and vertical envelopment became a potent tactic against which the insurgents had little defence. Such envelopment tactics were borrowed from French helicopter operations developed in Algeria, and this is the story of their refinement in African combat. In the following pages we will explore just how the Paras adapted to the African security environment and developed into a potent counterinsurgency force.

CHAPTER 1
THE BEGINNING

The Portuguese paratroopers (*Pára-quedistas*) or "Paras" began as a stepchild of the army and found a home in the Portuguese Air Force (*Força Aérea Portuguesa* or FAP) in 1955. Initially, the post-World War Two Portuguese Army seemed to have had mixed emotions about the need for elite, special-purpose forces that operated in small units with the attendant flexibility and elevated lethality. Shock troops have been traditionally controversial, and even the vaunted military theorist Baron Karl von Clausewitz saw little point in them. This attitude affected most modern general staff officers, regardless of nationality, and almost certainly encouraged their general opposition to irregular forces and unorthodox forms of warfare. The history of the Paras in the Portuguese Army is illustrative of this ambivalent view. Nevertheless, in a "war of the weak" in which insurgents avoid government strengths and exploit its vulnerabilities using agility, deception, and imagination, such small, crack government units are particularly well suited to counterinsurgency operations. This appreciation emerged with the advent of a new kind of war in Portuguese Africa, and Kaúlza de Arriaga, the Sub-secretary of State for Air at the time and a strategic thinker of the first order, well understood the potential of Paras when combined with the mobility of the helicopter. This vision would be realised on the African battlefield with devastating consequences for the enemy; however, jumping from aircraft did not immediately reveal this potential.

PIONEERS

The first parachute descents by Portuguese were made on 6 October 1922 by Captain Mário Costa França and Lieutenant José de Barros, both military engineers and respectively the first and second commanding officers of the Aerostatics Company (*Companhia de Aerosteiros*) located in Alverca. It was at the time the only aviation unit in the Portugal. The two officers jumped from a balloon at an altitude of 500 metres and landed safely.[1] Eight years later on 14 October 1930, Corporal José Maria da Veiga e Moura jumped from a Morane-Saulnier type H aircraft at 800 metres over the runways of Tancos using an Aviorex silk parachute and landed safely a kilometre northeast of the airfield in the village of Madeiras.[2] No further military parachuting occurred in Portugal or its possessions between this demonstration and the Japanese invasion of Portuguese Timor in February 1942.

Captain França (left) and Lieutenant Barros (right) following their successful jump at Alverca. Source *Archivo Histórico Militar*

TIMOR

Initial concern over a Japanese threat to Timor began much earlier in 1941, when the Dutch and Australian governments agreed to Australian reinforcements for West Timor, a part of the Dutch East Indies. Following the Japanese attack on Pearl Harbor on 7 December 1941, a 1,400-man detachment, designated Sparrow Force and centred on the 2/40th Battalion of the 8th Division of the Australian Army, was mobilised and arrived at Kupang, West Timor, on 12 December.[3] The situation in East Timor was different in that it was Portuguese territory. Portugal was neutral at the time and declined to cooperate with the Allies. Even so, Australia inserted a small force into the Portuguese territory composed of the 2/2nd Independent Company of 250 commandos and a small number of local Dutch forces to protect the eastern flank of Sparrow Force.[4] The modest Portuguese garrison in Dili, the capital, offered no resistance, and the local citizenry generally welcomed the troops. The Japanese began air bombardment of Timor on 26 January 1942 and landed the 228th Regimental Group, a part of the 38th Division, Imperial Japanese Army, in the early hours of 20 February. The Australian and Dutch forces in West Timor, isolated and overwhelmed, surrendered on 23 February. The 200-man remnant of Sparrow Force and about 200 Dutch East Indies troops found their way eastward into Portuguese territory and eventually joined the 2/2nd Independent Company. The 2/40th ceased to exist, and its survivors were absorbed into the 2/2nd.

When elements of the 228th Regimental Group made first contact with the Allied force in Dili, the capital, the 2/2nd Independent Company made the decision not to attempt suicidal engagement with a vastly superior force and began an orderly retreat towards the mountainous interior and the south coast. Suddenly the war on Timor had transitioned from a conventional conflict to a guerrilla war. The Australians now sought to mobilise the Timorese and Portuguese despite knowing nothing of them and not speaking their language. Nevertheless, these local people served alongside the Australians, became the eyes and ears of the force, hauled supplies and equipment to make it mobile and agile, gave the men food and shelter, and refused to inform on them.[5]

On Timor there was certainly an enormous dislike of the invaders and a consequent general resistance to their presence, for there is indeed a rich history of the Timorese assisting the 2/2nd independent Company and its augmentees. This began with the young *criados* or footmen, boys with an average age of about thirteen who served as loyal and indispensable guides, porters, and gathers of food and intelligence. Even entire tribes and clans were organised, armed, trained, and deployed by the Australians to fight against the Japanese.[6] Even so, with a Japanese force of some 12,000 working against the small force centred around the Australian commandos, the result was predictable, and the last Australians were evacuated by the submarine USS *Gudgeon* (SS-211) on 10 February 1943. From this date until the end of the war sixteen teams were recruited from Timorese, Portuguese, and Australians to return to Portuguese Timor and mobilise resistance to the Japanese occupation. If these teams and their progeny could preoccupy the Japanese, then the chances of a Japanese invasion of Australia would be diminished.

During the war there were over 600 Portuguese Timorese evacuated from Timor, and this population potentially represented a valuable recruiting pool for the clandestine Allied forces. As it evolved, about 100 of the evacuees served in the Services Reconnaissance Department (SRD), which was the special operations arm of the Australian Army.[7] Many of these received formal commando and parachute training and became operatives in the Z Special Unit of the SRD. Members of Z Special Unit wore Australian uniforms, carried Australian weapons, and served under Australian command when they returned to Portuguese Timor to fight. Few survived. Among these volunteers there were twelve young Timorese who completed parachute training at the 1st Parachute Training Centre, RAAF Richmond, New South Wales, and subsequently at RAAF Leyburn, Queensland. They are listed below with their ultimate disposition:[8]

José "Zeca" Rebelo: Disappeared in combat.
Armindo Fernandes: Captured by the Japanese, died in prison.
José de Carvalho: Captured by the Japanese, died in prison.
Celestino dos Anjos: Jumped into Timor on Operation SUNLAG and distinguished himself, decorated by Australian and Portuguese Governments for his service.
João de Almeida: Settled in Australia following the war.
Bernardino dos Reis Noronha: Settled in Australia following the war.
Câncio dos Reis Noronha: Settled in Australia following the war.
António José Álvaro Pinto: Settled in Australia following the war.
Abel Manuel de Sousa: Settled in Australia following the war.
Félix da Silva Barreto: Settled in Australia following the war.
João da Silva Bublic: Settled in Australia following the war.
José Joachim do Santos: Settled in Australia following the war.

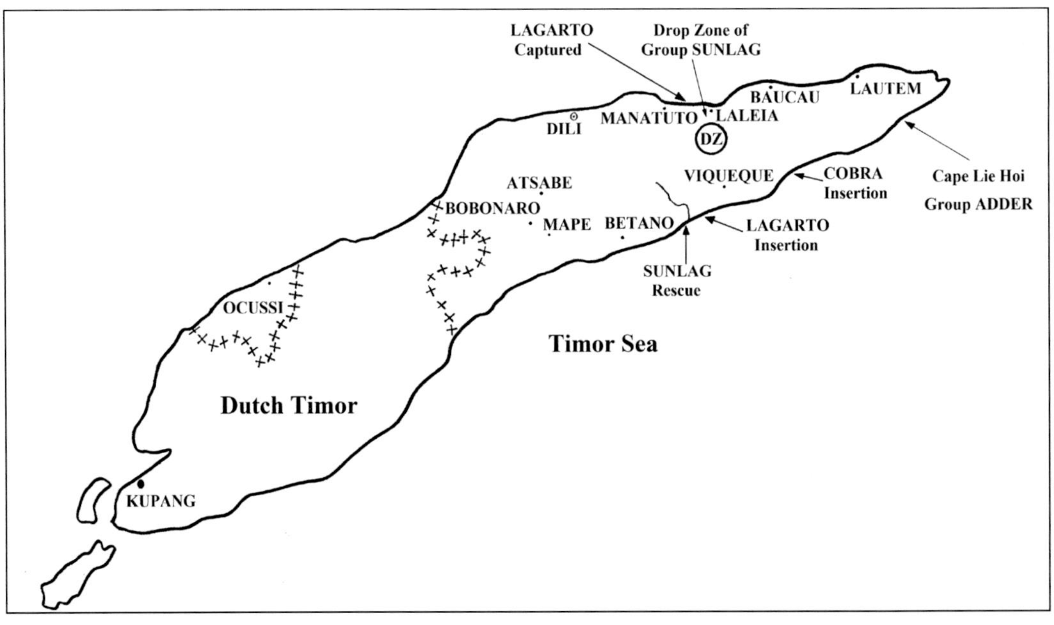

Timor showing the areas of infiltration of Operations ADDER and SUNLAG. (*Map by Luís A.M. Grão as modified by the author*)

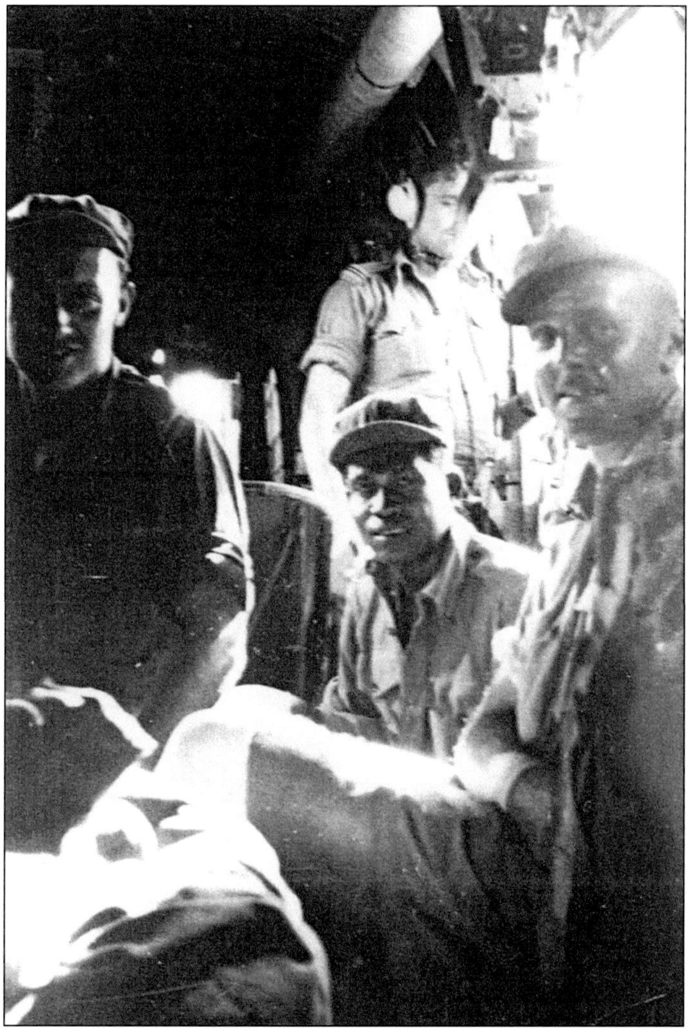

Photograph taken during Operation SUNLAG of the interior of a B-24 Liberator, No. 200 Flight RAAF, moments before the team's jump into Timor. Pictured are Sergeant Rod Dawson (left), Celestino dos Anjos (centre), and Captain Arthur Stevenson (right). The jumpmaster is beside the open door in the background. No. 200 Flight was a special duties flight of World War Two, formed in February 1945 to support the Allied Intelligence Bureau (AIB) and operated over Borneo, Timor, and the Dutch East Indies from March of that year until the end of the war in August. *(Source Archivo Histórico Militar)*

Félix Barreto on his completion of parachute training at RAAF Leyburn in April 1945. He is wearing the Australian Army parachute badge or "wings" on his left chest. *(Source Archivo Histórico Militar)*

The course for the Timorese began with intense physical preparation that included practicing parachute landing techniques and aircraft exit procedures. This training advanced to tower jumps and then actual airborne jumps first without equipment and then with the full complement of weapons, ammunition and all of the other paraphernalia needed to survive in Timor and be effective operatives. The final jumps involved water landings with rubber boats and life preservers.[9] Because the Timorese were civilians, additional training was needed on orientation instruction with compass, maps, and charts, weapons handling, Japanese aircraft and ship recognition, proficiency in Morse code and radio communication, and subversion and propaganda techniques.[10] At RAAF Richmond seven jumps were required to qualify. When training was transferred to RAAF Leyburn, the course was reduced to ten days of parachute-specific training with fewer jumps being required to qualify. Lieutenant Arthur Stevenson, Sergeant Rod Dawson, and Felix da Silva Barreto completed the Leyburn course in April 1945.[11] For the final phase of training, the candidates were relocated to Frazer Island, where all of the skills acquired earlier at Richmond or Leyburn were reinforced and intensified, particularly that of night-time land navigation.[12]

In the first SRD operations into Timor, personnel were infiltrated through beach landings from submarines or small naval vessels. The initial three operations styled LIZARD I, II, and III took place between 7 July 1942 and 10 February 1943 and were exclusively British and Australian exploratory forays with the help of Timorese guides to develop a feel for conditions following the invasion.[13] LIZARD II made contact with Lieutenant Manuel de Jesus Pires, the district administration for São Domingos, who helped the LIZARD operatives. LIZARD operations altogether managed to arm and train significant numbers of Timorese tribesmen:

> Groups of fifty natives were brought in at a time and given one week's training in elementary rifle use, followed by range practice. At the end of the course, they were capable of handling a rifle and firing with reasonable accuracy over 100 metres, a sufficient range in the type of country in which they would be fighting.[14]

On 10 February the LIZARD III force of six Australians and twenty-eight Timorese, including Pires, was evacuated by the USS *Gudgeon* (SS-211).[15]

There were now approximately sixty Portuguese and Timorese who continued the work of LIZARD under the name of PORTOLIZARD between 10 February and 4 August 1943 and reported from the Dilor River area on the south coast. As the Japanese continued to augment their forces on the island, conditions for PORTOLIZARD became increasingly difficult, and the force asked to be evacuated.

Meanwhile Pires was anxious to return, and this was arranged with the proviso that his operation LAGARTO would be under control of the SRD. His assignment was to create a clandestine network covering the eastern part of the country.[16] The LAGARTO party of four, which included Pires, Sergeant José Francisco Arranhado, Corporal Casimiro Augusto Paiva, and Patrício da Luz, arrived off East Timor on 28 July 1943 aboard the USS *Gar* (SS-206) but could not make contact with PORTOLIZARD. Pires elected to break radio silence three times to coordinate with PORTOLIZARD, and finally after four nights PORTOLIZARD appeared.[17] On 1 July the four disembarked late in the evening from the *Gar* at a *colião* or beachside lagoon between the Luca and Dilor Rivers and about twelve kilometres southwest of Viqueque; however, the evolution was not without its difficulties. Arranhado and Paiva argued with Pires on the viability of the operation and initially refused to go ashore. The commanding officer of the *Gar*, Lieutenant Commander Phillip Quirk, informed the SRD, which replied that those refusing orders would be interned for the duration of the war.[18] On this note, the LAGARTO four left *Gar* for the shore in a sixteen-foot canvas and wood boat with medicines, and some food supplies. As the group brought the boat to the beach through the rough surf, Pires lost his glasses, a suitcase, and three radios in the water. Quirk described Pires as "very poorly organised" and "almost completely blind and quite aged."[19] He was thirty-nine years at the time.

A number of PORTOLIZARD operatives were recruited for LAGARTO. The balance were evacuated by Royal Australian Navy (RAN) Fairmile motor launches on 4 and 5 August. An SRD operative, Sergeant James Ellwood, was inserted during the evacuation to assist Pires, who immediately resented his presence as interference.[20] LAGARTO under Pires's leadership expanded to thirty-four operatives, and developed into a relatively large and clumsy force stumbling through the mountainous jungle and leaving a highly visible footprint. This was hardly the small, covert commando force that had been successful earlier and reflected poorly on SRD training. Eventually the amateurish behaviour attracted enough Japanese attention that on 29 September LAGARTO was attacked, and Pires, Ellwood, and several Timorese were captured. Only Luz escaped.[21] Now under Japanese control, LAGARTO continued to send reports to SRD. It was only in mid-March 1945, some twenty months later, that SRD began to suspect that LAGARTO had been compromised.

In the meantime SRD was completely fooled by the Japanese deception operation and sent another four doomed missions:

- COBRA 27 January to mid-February 1944 Captured
- ADDER 21 and 22 August 1944 Captured
- SUNABLE 27 June to 12 July 1945 Captured
- SUNCOB 1 July to 17 July 1945 Captured

Neither LAGARTO nor COBRA seemed able to provide intelligence to SRD on the new Japanese airfields at Fuiloro or Lautem, so SRD initiated ADDER, which was put ashore at Cape Lie Hoi on 29 August 1944. The team of five was composed of two Australians and three Timorese:[22]

- Captain J. Grimson
- Sergeant E. Gregg
- Armindo da Conceição Fernandes
- Corporal José (Zeca) Rebelo
- José de Carvalho

The three Timorese had trained at Fraser Island and completed their parachute qualifications at RAAF Richmond. Sadly the morning after the landing Japanese troops engaged the group, and Grimson and Gregg were killed. Fernandes and Carvalho were captured and died in all likelihood from mistreatment, malnutrition, and disease.

Patrício Luz, the radioman in Operation LAGARTO and the only one of the party to escape, poses for a photograph after the war. (*Source Australian War Memorial, Sergeant K.B. Davis, photographer)*

Fairmile Motor Launch ML-815, which accompanied ML-814 on Operation LAGARTO. In SRD operations the depth charges were unloaded to provide extra deck space, and a special launching ramp was constructed over the stern to enable the rapid deployment of a large wooden and canvas landing craft. This craft was rowed inshore to effect the landing of stores and provisions and would subsequently return to the Fairmiles with the civilian evacuees or recovered operatives. (*Source Australian War Memorial*)

Rebelo apparently died after falling off a cliff eluding the enemy.[23] Each of the four missions suffered a short life, and the members of each group who survived engagement to be captured were forced to participate in the deception of SRD with fake messages.

By November 1944 there were 26,000 Japanese troops on Timor.[24] However, the war was not going well for Imperial Japan, and its troops were needed elsewhere. By August the Japanese force level had been reduced to between 6,000 and 8,000.[25]

Finally SRD, now suspicious of LAGARTO, proposed a mission to reinforce it and assembled a team of three operatives in April 1945: Captain Arthur Stevenson, Sergeant Rod Dawson, and the Timorese parachutist Celestinho dos Anjos, the son of a local *luirai* or king in the Viqueque area. Stevenson held dos Anjos in high regard, as they had both completed weapons and parachute training at RAAF Leyburn.[26] SRD styled the mission SUNLAG.

Stevenson suggested a plan to land in Timor unannounced and a day or so later from a concealed layup observe a proposed supply drop to LAGARTO. According to Stevenson's plan, the three operatives would parachute into Timor on 29 June 1945, position themselves to observe the sham night supply drop, and from their concealed position verify the compromise of LAGARTO. The party was dropped on the appointed date from a B-24 Liberator of the RAAF 200 Flight from 2,000 feet at dusk into the Laleta River area about twenty-one kilometres southeast of Manatuto. SRD advised LAGARTO that SUNLAG would be inserted on 1 July, two days after the fact. On this day the three SUNLAG operatives were positioned at the designated drop zone, and as as dusk turned to darkness, Stevenson heard a familiar clicking sound that he remembered from an earlier experience, the movement of Japanese soldiers who were silent except for the clicking sound of their bayonets rattling in their scabbards.[27] They passed within fifteen metres of Stevenson. Then Ellwood appeared, and Stevenson saw him as an obvious Australian, thin and pale, but seemingly in good health. He was escorted by two Japanese soldiers and carried a Lucas lamp for signalling to the aircraft. The operatives watched the enemy until 2130 hours, when he departed after waiting in vain for a drop that was never to come.[28]

The next day SUNLAG began its move south toward the coast and its anticipated extraction point but soon discovered that the countryside had become "a maze of sentry posts manned by Timorese militia."[29] Stevenson's radio temporarily failed, and he was unable to confirm to SRD the compromised state of LAGARTO until 3 July, the day after the launching of another ill-fated mission, SUNCOB.[30]

After three days of dodging militia in difficult terrain, the entire party's boots were worn out and useless. Progress was laboured. Meanwhile, SRD attempted to arrange an extraction on the south coast, but after four attempts to make contact, the ship returned to Australia. After three weeks of eluding the Japanese and foraging, the party was desperate. On 22 July dos Anjos took the risk of going to his village of Bibileo and successfully returned with chicken and corn, but soon word spread, and the group was compromised. The Japanese now pursued the three with infantry, militia, and dogs, but SUNLAG was able to evade successfully and positioned itself on the south coast in anticipation of a rendezvous. Finally it was arranged for 5 August, and a Fairmile took Stevenson, dos Anjos, and a barely conscious Dawson on board. Sadly Dawson died of kidney failure five days after his return to Darwin.[31]

Despite the compromise of many SRD operations, the Timorese operatives, Portugal's first paratroopers in combat, were loyal to their country of East Timor and to the Australians. Sadly their selfless devotion to duty in the face of extreme danger has largely remained a forgotten corner of World War Two. On the other hand, the Australian Army learned many lessons from its Timor operations and adapted its special operations training from its experiences in Timor. These included food and sleep deprivation to push a candidate to his breaking point and test his leadership and judgment. A food ration was offered only once every two days, and a candidate was lucky to get three hours of broken sleep a night. The most punishing aspect of all for the candidates was their not knowing when their training would end.[32] Similar methods would be introduced by the Portuguese in training their elite forces for Africa.

INTERWAR YEARS

Following World War Two and the success of both the German airborne forces in Crete and the Allied airborne forces in Normandy, it was thought that Portugal ought to explore the idea of developing its own paratrooper capability by sending some men from the army to be trained abroad. Accordingly, in August 1951 two infantry officers out of four volunteers were selected: Captains Martins Videira and Monteiro Robalo. They were sent to Pau, France, to the *École des*

The practice jump tower at Pau where the initial group of volunteers trained. *Source Archivo Histórico Militar*):

Landing instruction for the Portuguese volunteers at Pau. *Source Archivo Histórico Militar*)

Troupes Aeroportées (ETAP) to undergo the French parachute training course. Unlike the Australian training, which covered the broader spectrum of warfare, this course taught only the techniques of parachuting. Progress toward qualification included ground training and practice, and daylight and night-time jumps, but excluded any disciplines related to the military employment of Paras. The two officers returned in November of the same year "breveted" as Paras and wearing their French parachute qualification badge. They rejoined their units, where they continued their duties as before with no ability to maintain their newly found qualifications.[33]

The paratrooper idea limped along with additional volunteers attending both parachute and instructor/monitor courses between August and December 1953. Several volunteers likewise attended the parachute and instructor/monitor courses at the Military School of Parachutists (*Escuela Militar de Paracaidistas* or EMP) in Alcantarilla, Spain, and returned at the end of March 1954.[34] There was now a total of eight qualified Paras in the Portuguese Army.[35]

The FAP had been established in 1952, and the relevant Decree Law No. 2055 doing so made reference to the paratroopers and the need to integrate their training and operations into the FAP. Meanwhile, the army continued to debate over the creation of one or more parachute units. Still by 1954, the eight trained parachutists remained scattered throughout the army and had not been formed into their own specialised unit. Their skills were atrophying through bureaucratic indecision, and Arriaga, citing the relevant Decree Law, argued in 1955 that the FAP should have the paratrooper portfolio and develop it as an elite force of airborne shock troops.[36] Because these were to be light infantry, and the FAP was not the army, there was still much debate. Would these troops belong to the FAP until they were on the ground, and then come under army control? The question was settled by the Minister of National Defence, who lodged the paratroopers with the FAP but limited the force to a single battalion.[37]

With this development, the FAP grasped the initiative and took steps to create a proper battalion of paratroopers. Its first move occurred at the beginning of 1955, when it called for volunteers for paratrooper training. About 1,500 candidates responded from the three service branches, and from these, 232 were considered qualified and sent for training at Alcantarilla, as Portugal had neither the needed competences nor the infrastructure for paratrooper training at the time. These candidates were put under the command of Captain Videira and assembled at Campo de Tiro da Serra da Carregueira, where they prepared for their course in Spain. Each candidate received a new and distinctive "paratrooper" uniform of superior quality made to measure by a Lisbon tailor. This decision to furnish all of the volunteers with the same unique uniform was aimed at instilling a particular esprit de corps for those who would become the future "green berets" of Portugal.

Once in Spain, the volunteers adapted rapidly to the rhythm of instruction and were soon sharing jumps with the Spanish army and air force paratroopers. By July the three-month course, the 22nd for the EMP, was completed, and 188 of the volunteers were awarded their Spanish paratrooper badges.[38]

On their return to the Campo de Tiro da Serra da Carregueira with their new green berets, these graduates of the "Spanish Course" began to establish a proper training regimen to expand their numbers to battalion strength. Young, innovative, and enthusiastic, these Paras were creating a new military unit completely filled by volunteers and endowed with a spirit that made them the "troops that all of the others sought to imitate."[39] This was the foundation of the new parachute battalion (*Batalhão de Caçadores Pára-quedistas* or BCP).

Newly designed paratrooper uniform for a paratroop aspirant with the forage cap. (*Source Museu das Tropas Pára-quedistas, drawing by José Rodrigues*)

Newly designed paratroop uniform for a designated paratrooper wearing the beret. (*Source Museu das Tropas Pára-quedistas, drawing by José Rodrigues*)

At Alcantarilla in 1955, Captain Videira gives encouragement to his paratrooper students prior to a jump. (*Source Museu das Tropas Pára-quedistas*)

Following the training in Spain, the BCP in its skeletal state was presented to the nation in a formal ceremony in 14 August 1955 and paraded on the Avenida da Liberdade in Lisbon before the President of the Republic, General Craveiro Lopes. Lopes inspected

At Alcantarilla a Portuguese student boards a Spanish Junkers Ju-52 for a jump. The Ju-52 held fourteen paratroopers. (*Source Museu das Tropas Pára-quedistas*)

Portuguese paratrooper students march at Alcantarilla in their student uniforms with the forage caps. (*Source Museu das Tropas Pára-quedistas*)

At Alcantarilla aircraft exit practice from a platform onto a trampoline. (*Source Museu das Tropas Pára-quedistas*)

Captain Videira receives the BCP standard from General Craveiro Lopes, President of the Republic. (*Source Direcção-Geral da Comunicação Social*)

the formation before the parade and presented Captain Videira with the standard of the BCP in a moving ceremony.[40]

Next the BCP moved to its new quarters adjacent to the air base at Tancos and shortly thereafter on 15 October made its first jump over its new home from a Junker Ju-52 transport aircraft. This exercise represented the beginning of a centre of instruction at Tancos for the continued proficiency and expansion of the Paras. Over the next several years the BCP broadened its training and capabilities to the point that it was ready for deployment as a frontline unit of the Portuguese armed forces. The training too was formalised and remained unchanged until 1971. In sequence it consisted of twelve weeks of recruit training, four weeks of parachute training, and eleven weeks of combat instruction. In 1971, the order of training was altered in that the combat instruction was conducted before the parachute training.[41]

Its organisation was formalised with two companies of Paras, one company of support, and a fourth of instruction.[42] This represented a force strength of twenty-three officers, forty-five sergeants, and four hundred seventeen Paras. As the unit was new and experimental, novel ideas were constantly being explored. One was the adoption of a camouflage battle dress based on the French pattern. Another

The BCP parades before the President of the Republic as a part of its presentation to the people of Portugal. *(Source Direcção-Geral da Comunicação Social)*

French parachute qualification badge. (*Source Museu das Tropas Pára-quedistas*)

Spanish parachute qualification badge. (*Source Museu das Tropas Pára-quedistas*)

Portuguese parachute qualification badge. (*Source Museu das Tropas Pára-quedistas*)

Portuguese paratroop beret insignia. (*Source Museu das Tropas Pára-quedistas*)

Captain Videira (left), commanding officer of the BCP, and Captain Robalo (right). (*Source Museu das Tropas Pára-quedistas*)

Junkers Ju-52 embarking Paras in Tancos for a training jump. (*Source Museu das Tropas Pára-quedistas*)

Combat dogs on parade with their para handlers. (*Source Museu das Tropas Pára-quedistas*)

Exercise HIMBA, Paras arriving at the Luanda Airport for Exercise HIMBA. (*Source Museu das Tropas Pára-quedistas*)

Douglas C-54 Skymasters in Luanda awaiting Paras for their drops in Exercise HIMBA. (*Source personal collection of General Tomás George da Conceição Silva*)

Paras awaiting embarkation for a jump in Exercise HIMBA. (*Source Museu das Tropas Pára-quedistas*)

was the establishment of a Centre of Instruction for Combat Dogs. In the fall of 1958, BCP officers were sent to the United Kingdom to complete the British Army commando course. The BCP was also up-armed with the acquisition of rifle grenades and rocket-propelled grenades (RPG). By 1959, and BCP was indeed a potent organisation, and Arriaga was prepared to put it on display in Africa.

EXERCISE HIMBA

In step with the augmentation of the FAP in the *ultramar*, Arriaga and his staff conceived of Exercise HIMBA (Lion). This was an air transport exercise in which the BCP would be loaded on transports and sent to Angola, where power projection would be demonstrated by several air drops at key cities. There were fourteen aircraft participating:

Paras embarking on a C-54 in preparation for their demonstration jump in Exercise HIMBA. (*Source Museu das Tropas Pára-quedistas*)

Paras readying for a jump during Operation HIMBA. (*Source Museu das Tropas Pára-quedistas*)

The RCP parading in the Baixa in Lisbon. (*Source Museu das Tropas Pára-quedistas*)

Paras parading in the centre of Luanda following their demonstration jump in Exercise HIMBA. (*Source Museu das Tropas Pára-quedistas*)

Kaúlza de Arriaga (centre) arriving for Exercise HIMBA flanked by General Venâncio Augusto Deslandes (left), commander of the armed forces of Angola, and Brigadier Fernando Pinto de Resende (right), commander of the Angolan air region. (*Source personal collection of General Tomás George da Conceição Silva*)

Six	PV-2	Harpoons from BA 6 (Montijo)
Three	SC-54	Skymasters from BA 4 (Lajes, Azores)
Four	C-47	Dakotas from AB 1 (Lisbon)
One	C-47	Dakota from BA 3 (Tancos)
One	Company of the BCP embarked in a C-54.	

Unfortunately, the beginning of the exercise was marred by a tragic accident in which a C-47 crashed shortly after takeoff from Lisbon and went into the Tagus River with the loss of all aboard and the payroll for the entire exercise. The remaining fleet of aircraft flew to Luanda by way of Guiné and São Tomé on 30 April, and once in Luanda, flew to Nova Lisboa and Sá da Bandeira, where in each case the company jumped and then conducted a parade. Returning to Luanda, the paratroops participated in an air festival and concluded the exercise.

Douglas C-47 Dakota being loaded on the ramp at Luanda. (*Source personal collection of General Tomás George da Conceição Silva*)

Lockheed PV-2 Harpoon aircraft on the ramp at Luanda. (*Source personal collection of General Tomás George da Conceição Silva*)

The entire exhibition was an unqualified success despite the tragic loss of the C-47. The Paras were received joyously by the people of Angola and were truly impressive both in action and on parade. Indeed, in looking back on the exercise, one journalist observed in a halo of emotion that the expanded presence of the FAP in Angola represented a modern Lusitanian link with the *metrópole*.[43]

Enthusiastic about the success of Exercise HIMBA, Arriaga in the spring of 1959 ordered the planning of a similar mission for Mozambique with the code name Exercise IBIS. It would require twenty aircraft and 800 paratroopers.[44] Over the next several months it became apparent that Mozambique was not prepared to accommodate an exercise of this size. The airfield infrastructure was largely undeveloped, and it would consequently take time to improve the existing ones and to build new ones. The logistics infrastructure also was not in place for any large-scale deployment of air units, and it needed to be built. In light of these shortcomings, the exercise was postponed until September or October 1960.[45] Again, after much consideration, the exercise was targeted for April 1961, the beginning of the dry season. Airfield and logistics problems were not the only obstacles, as the relatively large number of aircraft required posed a further hurdle. To assemble these would necessitate borrowing aircraft from TAP, the Portuguese national airline, and cancelling Portuguese participation in concurrent NATO exercises, both fairly extreme measures. Ultimately it was shelved.

In January 1960, BCP force strength was reset at forty-four officers, eighty-two sergeants, and six hundred Paras.[46] In the summer of 1960 a select group of officers, sergeants, and Paras were sent to France and Algeria, where they completed the French Army course on revolutionary war that specialised in counterinsurgency and psychological operations.

Captain Videira in Algeria with the French "Paras." *Source Museu das Tropas Pára-quedistas*)

DEVELOPMENTS IN THE *ULTRAMAR*

Beginning in 1947 with the independence of India, Great Britain began the dissolution of its Empire. After two unsatisfactory colonial wars, one in Indochina and the other in Algeria, France dismantled its Empire. Portugal was now the remaining colonial power. Its position was very different from Britain and France in that it had been in Africa since the beginning of the fifteenth century, over four and a half centuries and longer by far than any other colonial power. It considered its overseas territories, known as the *ultramar*, an integral part of continental Portugal and refused to consider granting independence to them. Its commitment to their defence had its origins not only in their long-term ownership but also in their economic promise and the inflexible African policy of Dr. António Salazar, the prime minister. With the progressive decline of its trading position in the Indian Ocean beginning in 1578, the loss of its colony of Brazil in 1822, and the missed opportunity of a coast-to-coast possession in austral Africa in 1890, the only potential of the Empire lay in the large but incompletely developed colonies of Angola and Mozambique. These in Portuguese minds held the promise of a renewed prosperity and greatness. Further, with the heritage of having been Portuguese for so long, their ownership was to be defended at all costs. For this small European nation, the importance of the colonies was captured in an editorial by Dr. Marcello Caetano in *O Mundo Português* (Portuguese World) that appeared in 1935: "Africa is for us a moral justification and a *raison d'être* as a power. Without it we would be a small nation; with it, we are a great country."[47] The growth of revolutionary climate in the *ultramar* during the 1950s clashed with this philosophy and the country's refusal to break the colonial bond and to decolonise. The "winds of change" were blowing through Africa, but the Salazar regime refused to consider holding democratic elections or decolonising.

Political opposition to Salazar and his policies was tolerated neither at home nor in the *ultramar*. Thus an explosion was inevitable, and when it happened in 1961, the events in Angola and the seizing of Goa by India pushed Salazar to solidify the Portuguese commitment to defend the remaining colonies. So strong was this feeling that it defied any voice of reason and foreclosed any retreat or compromise over African affairs. The Portuguese armed forces and treasure were thus pledged in full to preserve its Empire and the potential of renewed prosperity through an expensive counterinsurgency campaign. Developments in the Congo foretold an assault on the north of Angola.

CONGO ANARCHY AND INDEPENDENCE

The Belgian Congo had prospered, since its transfer to the Belgian government from the estate of its King Leopold II in 1908. It now operated under a colonial ministry that answered to a democratically elected parliament that had opened the heretofore crown domains to private ownership and had ended its monopoly on trade. The right of the Congolese to own and work their lands had been restored. The system of forced labour had been abolished. As a consequence of these new liberalisations came new opportunities. The European population moved to take advantage of the potential in the Congo, and its numbers there had risen from about 3,000 in 1908 to more than 100,000 in 1960.[48] There occurred over this period a great rush of development in agriculture, banking, mining, and infrastructure. Despite all of this apparent progress and its attendant social benefits, there remained a strong undercurrent of resentment within the local population. No civil rights for the Congolese were thought necessary, and racial segregation was standard practice. The highest rank a Congolese could hold in the colonial administration was one of a minor clerk in the civil service or a non-commissioned officer in the Congolese army, known as the *Force Publique*. Until 1955 the Congolese were forbidden to attend college and even after that could only attend designated institutions so as not to be "corrupted." When independence came in 1960, there were fewer than thirty African university graduates. Of the 5,000 management-level positions in the civil service, only three were filled by Africans.[49]

Despite the democratic government of Belgium, the Congo since 1908 had been run by decree from Brussels through a governor-general in its capital, Léopoldville. The colony was permitted no politicians, no political parties, and no elections.[50] No Congolese or Belgians residing there had a vote on any matter. Following World War Two and the subsequent political developments in the neighbouring French and British colonies, Belgium was obliged in 1956 to permit the same political freedom in the Congo. Prior to that time there had been social, religious, and cultural clubs formed along regional and tribal lines. Within this framework there were discussions on how the Congolese might improve their plight and ultimately gain independence. These clubs now became the political parties of the Congo. By late 1959 the activities of these various political movements had matured to a point of demanding independence. The MNC (*Mouvement National Congolais* or Congolese National Movement), founded in October 1958 by the charismatic postal clerk Patrice Lumumba, had grown out of a government workers' club in Stanleyville. ABAKO (*Alliance des Ba-Kongo* or Alliance of the Bacongo), the powerful cultural-political association of the Bakongo people, was led by Joseph Kasabuvu, a pudgy civil servant who became its president in 1955. CONAKAT (*Confédération des Associations Tribales du Katanga* or Confederation of the Tribal Associations of Katanga) was a former club among the Luba-Lunda tribesmen founded by Moise Tshombe. The leader of a soldiers' club in the *Force Publique* garrison at Thysville was a young sergeant-major, Joseph-Désiré Mobutu.

Beginning in January 1959, these demands for immediate independence were reinforced by rallies and strikes, many violent and bloody. By October, the violence and tension had reached a level not seen since the time of Livingstone some ninety years earlier. Tribal conflict with painted warriors and dismembered cadavers, displays of religious fanaticism, the airing of latent grievances, all of these added to the strikes and rallies and caused hundreds of dead and injured.[51] This mayhem created a sense of urgency within the Belgian government and caused it to rethink its colonial policy of a five-year transition culminating in 1964. Tribal rivalries and agitation persisted and prompted the Belgians to clarify the political evolution and consider an African government in nine months.[52] This reconsideration was shortened by a month and formalised at the February 1960 Round Table Conference in Brussels, at which it was resolved to grant the Congo its independence in June, a mere four months hence. This generous concession was an attempt to satisfy the Congolese political leaders, who wanted immediate independence and wished to ascend to power without having to consult the people.[53]

In this short period the Belgian government attempted to overcome the enormous obstacles of accelerating the formation of a new Congolese government, a patently impossible task. It left little time for the Congolese to organise themselves politically, hold a wide array of elections, and assume the colonial administration from the Belgians using the largely untrained and uneducated local population. The seeds of immediate trouble began during the election campaign, in which candidates made wild promises, took the opportunity to vent long-repressed hostilities toward Europeans, and further stirred long-standing tribal animosities. Peter Forbath describes the scene leading to Independence Day as one of nervous excitement with crowds roaming the streets of major cities, "impatient for the miracles of freedom to begin, nursing tribal grudges, eager to become lords over the whites and take vengeance for past injustices."[54] In the 23 June elections, Patrice Lumumba's party outpolled Joseph Kasabuvu's; however, neither side could form a parliamentary coalition. Consequently, as a compromise measure they formed an uneasy partnership with Kasabuvu as president and Lumumba as prime minister. This fragile government might have survived in a benign environment; however, it stood little chance with the legacy bequeathed to it by Brussels. The mood rapidly degenerated and turned ugly during the first week of independence. Public services deteriorated with the wholesale departure of Belgian civil servants and a lack of trained Congolese to replace them. When the new civil servants were not paid, there were strikes that turned into riots when the *Force Publique* attempted to intervene. All semblance of order, however, vanished when the *Force Publique* itself mutinied, spawning a widespread wave of violence. Blacks attacked whites and each other, as they vented their anti-European hatreds and intertribal rivalries.

On 12 July, Lumumba asked for UN help, and three days later the first of 25,000 UN troops arrived. When Lumumba declared martial law, the political situation degenerated completely. The people of the lower Congo demanded the abolition of the central government in favour of a system of independent provincial governments. This demand was followed by a declaration of independence in Kasai Province. Lumumba's country was falling apart with good reason, and having no reliable way to enforce his will, he turned to the UN with a request to use its peace-keeping troops to unify the Congo by force. When it refused, he countered by appealing to the Soviet Union. It obliged with a flight of nineteen Ilyushin transport aircraft, thereby supplying sufficient arms and airlift capability to enable Lumumba to march on Kasai and pour the proverbial gasoline onto an already incendiary situation. In what Mike Hoar describes as a one-sided battle, Lumumba's forces massacred Kasai tribesmen by the hundreds in what was essentially a venting of ancient tribal animosities.[55]

At this point Lumumba was a spent force in any attempt to unify the Congo politically. While he was a persuasive orator, he proved to be an unstable diplomat and an incompetent head of state. On 5 September, Kasabuvu dismissed the prime minister. In turn Lumumba dismissed the president. Kasabuvu prevailed by placing Lumumba under house arrest with the support of Mobutu, now a colonel and head of the army. All pretence of a functioning government seems to have ended. On hearing of Lumumba's arrest and the ensuing confusion, Antoine Gizenga declared the secession of Oriental Province, Lumumba's power base with its capital in Stanleyville. Gizenga's forces attacked Mobutu's garrisons, and a new bout of the most brutal savagery raged through the rain forests. It involved the worst sort of tribal warfare marked by wholesale massacres and cannibalism.[56] In the midst of the anarchy, Mobutu formed a "college of administrators" on 14 September and assumed the day-to-day running of the government, "neutralising" all politicians. One of his first actions was to close the embassies of the Soviet Union and Czechoslovakia and banish their presence from the Congo.[57]

The situation stabilised for a time; however, in November, Lumumba left Léopoldville, where he had enjoyed UN protection, to travel to Stanleyville, where his supporters had control. En route he was caught on 2 December by Mobutu's troops, and on 17 January 1961 was flown to Katanga, where he was reluctantly received by Tshombe in an apparent near-death condition.[58] Later in the month he was shot while allegedly trying to escape from a rather dreadful mud hut in which he had been held prisoner.[59]

Lumumba's death caused an international outrage and raised the man to martyr-hero status. Mobutu returned the government to Kasabuvu, as his suspected hand in Lumumba's death became known, and in turn Kasabuvu made him commander-in-chief of the armed forces. The agony of the Congo continued until a better prepared Mobutu stepped in again in 1965 and ruled for better or for worse until his downfall and death in 1997. It is estimated that over 200,000 Congolese perished in the five years between independence and Mobutu's ascent. Hélio Felgas, a Portuguese Army major and Governor of the District of the Congo next to the Congo frontier, foresaw the threat from the Belgian Congo in this mayhem and in a report dated November 1959 urgently warned Portuguese authorities to prepare for spillover trouble.[60] Arriaga was one who took this warning very seriously and in January 1961 expanded the structure of the BCP to 1,390 enlisted personnel.[61] Likewise the term of enlistment was set at four years, of which twenty-four months would be spent in either Angola or Mozambique, or a combination of the two, or eighteen months in Guiné.[62]

ANGOLAN NATIONALIST MOVEMENTS

Following World War Two, nationalist sentiments grew among the *mestiços* (mixed-race peoples) and *assimilados* (mostly *mestiços* who were legally assimilated into Portuguese culture). However, these groups were largely urban and thus did not represent the greater population. As they were located in cities, they were in a hostile environment for two reasons: the majority of their opponents, the white population, lived in cities, and the national police or PIDE (*Polícia Internacional de Defesa do Estado*, or International Police for Defence of the State) operated most effectively there. Consequently, they were either short-lived or dormant.[63] By 1956 the young Marxists of the Angolan Communist Party contributed to the formation of the MPLA (*Movimento Popular de Libertação de Angola*, or Popular Movement for the Liberation of Angola). The MPLA developed roots among the urban and largely radical intellectuals of Luanda, among its slum dwellers, and to a lesser extent, eastward from the capital among the Mbundu, the second largest ethnolinguistic group in Angola, and the Chokwe people. These urban roots were composed largely of *mestiços*, who controlled the party. The movement had little in common with the rural peasants of the east and south of Angola and made little effort to gain their true devotion. In December 1956 the initial MPLA manifesto was openly published in a direct frontal assault on the government. Predictably the PIDE reacted adversely, and a number of the MPLA leaders were forced to flee into exile. From 1957 onward PIDE action was so successful "that the nationalists were not able to maintain more than the most rudimentary organisation inside the colonies and could not communicate with those cells that did exist."[64] The parties were forced to conduct their affairs from neighbouring states and were deeply influenced by their foreign connections.

The MPLA in exile established itself initially in Léopoldville but found itself in competition with the other prominent Angolan nationalist group at the time, the UPA (*Uniao das Populações de Angola*, or Union of Angolan Peoples), for acceptance as the leading representative of the Angolan people. In 1962 the MPLA formed its military wing, EPLA (*Exército Popular de Libertação de Angola*, or Popular Army for the Liberation of Angola), to project its influence into Angola. This nascent force numbered between 250 and 300 young men who had undergone military training in Ghana and Morocco. The EPLA sought to expand the conflict across the northern border of Angola with this force and penetrate the entire country, publicising the MPLA manifesto. Recruiting proved to be difficult because of ethnic rivalries, and military action was thwarted by the competing UPA. The UPA through its influence with the Congo leadership forced the MPLA to leave Léopoldville in 1963 and re-establish itself in Brazzaville, from which it was difficult to conduct a campaign across an unenthusiastic third country and into a now distant Angola. As a result northern Angola proved to be barren for the MPLA, and it was not until 1966, with the opening of its second front from Zambia, that some success would come.

The UPA was formed by Barros Nekaka in the mid-1950s from a number of small groups and in 1958 he passed leadership to his nephew Holden Roberto. UPA strength rested in the rural populations of the Bakongo ethnolinguistic region of Angola. These people straddled the border area that reached into the Belgian Congo, Angola, Cabinda and the French Congo, the footprint of the ancient Kongo kingdom. Roberto unequivocally held the view that not just a "Bakongo kingdom" or some other entity but all of Angola must be freed. An ardent anticolonialist, Roberto had been born in Angola but had lived his adult life in the Belgian Congo. He had been educated in the Baptist Church missionaries and employed in the Belgian colonial economy as an accountant between 1941 and 1949. The UPA was able to develop a following in the north of Angola because of the relatively open frontier, and this loyal cadre became the basis for the uprising in March 1961, of which we will hear more shortly. Portuguese presence in this area took the form of *chefes do posto* (heads of posts) and administrators, as opposed to PIDE, and these officials were so sparse that it was physically impossible for them to maintain anything but the most casual control over their districts.[65]

When the Belgian Congo became independent on 30 June 1960, its new government began to give Roberto practical assistance, including permission to establish a radio station and a training camp within its borders. This sanctuary was an important facet of UPA operations in its early years. Roberto had witnessed the long series of Congolese crises that had begun with the violent political rioting on 4 January 1959 and had led to the accelerated Belgian push toward Congo self-government and independence in eighteen months. By December 1960, he believed that just as the Belgians had quickly grown weary of armed conflict, so would the Portuguese when it was initiated. He consequently used his Congo sanctuary and the porous common border to set the stage for an end to relative colonial tranquillity for Portugal.

The UPA formed its military wing, the ELNA (*Exército de Libertação Nacional de Angola*, or Army of National Liberation of Angola), in June 1961 after the March attacks did not achieve a Portuguese withdrawal. The South African Defence Force vice-consul in Luanda, Brigadier Willem S. van der Waals, noted that the ELNA "involved itself in military activities in the narrowest sense...but avoided contact with the Portuguese security forces as far as possible."[66] Van der Waals further argues that in the traditional exercise of the informational lever of national power, Portuguese propaganda and social work among the refugees returning to Angola after the March 1961 attacks persuaded most of these displaced people to move into controlled settlements or *aldeamentos*. This development deprived the ELNA of popular support, and its military action consequently occurred in a human desert. It was thus unable to proselytise the population, as in a classic insurgency, and as an alternative focused on preventing competitive MPLA infiltration. It had also neglected to indoctrinate, organise, and win recruits among refugees in the Congo returning to Angola and had thus missed an important opportunity to undermine Portuguese authority. Thus despite its expansion to 6.200 troops, the ELNA had no internal political infrastructure in Angola.[67] Portugal gained the upper hand and dominated the human terrain until 1974 in a classic example of successful informational warfare with civil support and population proselytising.

This lack of direction caused great rifts in the UPA leadership. Despite the UPA reorganisation in March 1962 at the behest of Mobutu, now president of the Republic of the Congo, to include additional groups, to rename itself FNLA (*Frente Nacional de Libertção de Angola*, or National Front for the Liberation of Angola), and to establish a government in exile named GRAE (*Governo da República de Angola no Exílio*, or Government of the Republic of Angola in Exile), little of substance was accomplished. A frustrated Jonas Savimbi, Roberto's "foreign minister" and an Ovimbundu, formally broke with the UPA/FNLA in July 1964, labelling Roberto a "corrupt racist," and eventually formed the third nationalist movement in Angola, UNITA (*União Nacional para a Independência Total de Angola*, or the National Union for the Total Independence of Angola). Savimbi had publically announced his break at the 1964 Organisation of African Unity (OAU, now the African Union or AU) meeting in Cairo, Egypt, and alleged that Roberto had set up a "commercial empire in the Congo."[68] Within two years, Savimbi had built his meagre twelve-man force into a sizeable army, gaining popularity and support as the only leader to work within the country alongside his men in battle against the Portuguese. "Leaders must fight alongside the people and not stay abroad, sending 'second-class' fighters to face the Portuguese," Savimbi proclaimed as he denounced Roberto.[69] While Roberto was renowned for his aloofness, the bearded Savimbi mixed often and easily with ordinary people as well as his military. The next year Alexandre Taty, "minister of armaments," after challenging Roberto in an unsuccessful coup, defected to the Portuguese in Cabinda with a substantial number of his followers.

As the Portuguese weekly *Expresso* observed in 1974, "The FNLA is Holden Roberto and Holden Roberto belongs to Mobutu, to whom he is connected by an umbilical cord."[70] Mobutu was playing both ends against the middle in loudly proclaiming his support for the FNLA while discretely cultivating good relations with Portugal, for like Zambia, the Congo depended on the Benguela Railroad (CFB), which carried more than half of its foreign trade. There were also dissident elements in Angola that, if unleashed in cross-border operations, could make considerable trouble for him. Consequently he kept a tight control over the FNLA activities both within the Congo and without. He provided just enough political and material support to give it international credibility and to provide the Congo with a stake in Angola should the Portuguese eventually leave.[71] The Portuguese, it seems, had little to fear from Roberto and his organisation after the March 1961 attacks.

ASSAULT ON THE NORTH

The UPA assault on the north of Angola occurred primarily in the districts of Zaire, Uíge, and Cuanza Norte. The first two are next to the border, and the third contains the impenetrable Dembos region, a mountainous jungle area where UPA elements hid and prepared for the internal assault. During the weeks leading to 15 March, the UPA carefully prepared its assault plan, infiltrating agitators from the Congo. It assembled its forces not only on the frontier and in the Dembos but also in many different locales within the targeted regions and was able to do so largely in secret because of the remoteness of the area and the uncontrolled borders.[72]

The order to attack was described in a pamphlet widely disseminated to the population and marked the "beginning of the festival" as 15 March.[73] It cryptically ordered all those "followers to clean all *postos* thoroughly, and to treat the *chefs de posto* and their families and other whites well," and only some days later was the hostile intent of this message understood by the Portuguese authorities.[74] Another UPA document dated March 1961, Léopoldville, and titled "Rules to Follow for the Population of Angola in the Days of the Feast," reinforces the festival pamphlet and outlines specific procedures to be followed in the "celebrations."[75] It talks about women and children leaving their villages to participate in the celebrations, soldiers and sepoys allying with the people and joining the celebrations, and all people uniting in the success of the celebrations. The "celebrations," of course, were the intended acts of mayhem to destroy the agricultural commerce of the area and important communications infrastructure. These acts were described as "cleaning the farms" and the "destruction of bridges." The underlying logic in this plan was deeply flawed in that the population that was supposed to rise up and join the UPA forces depended for its survival on the prosperity of the farms and estates and the ability of these enterprises to get their crops to market by way of the interconnecting infrastructure. Thus despite their grievances, the resident population's loyalties could never ultimately lie with the UPA in this venture, and the people knew it.

The attacks were launched on signal, and the UPA attackers—an armed mob estimated to be 4,000 to 5,000 and drugged with *quimbombo* or *cacharama*, a native alcoholic drink and hyperstimulant, and convinced that they were immune to the white man's bullets—swarmed from their redoubts in the Congo, the Dembos, and elsewhere in the early morning hours of 15 March.[76] This figure was expanded by an estimated 25,000 through forced recruiting.[77] From the Congo, they crossed the border at approximately seven points along a 300-kilometer front in the area of São Salvador and moved south. Approximately 700 European farms and estates, additional trading settlements, and over 100 government administrative posts were overwhelmed.[78] The mob acted with refined cruelty in massacring men, women, black, white, young, and old. At 1230 hours on that day, Radio Brazzaville announced that "the rebel forces of the UPA had begun the fight for the independence of Angola, having decimated hundreds of whites."[79] At the same time that the sad news became known in Lisbon, there was great satisfaction in its

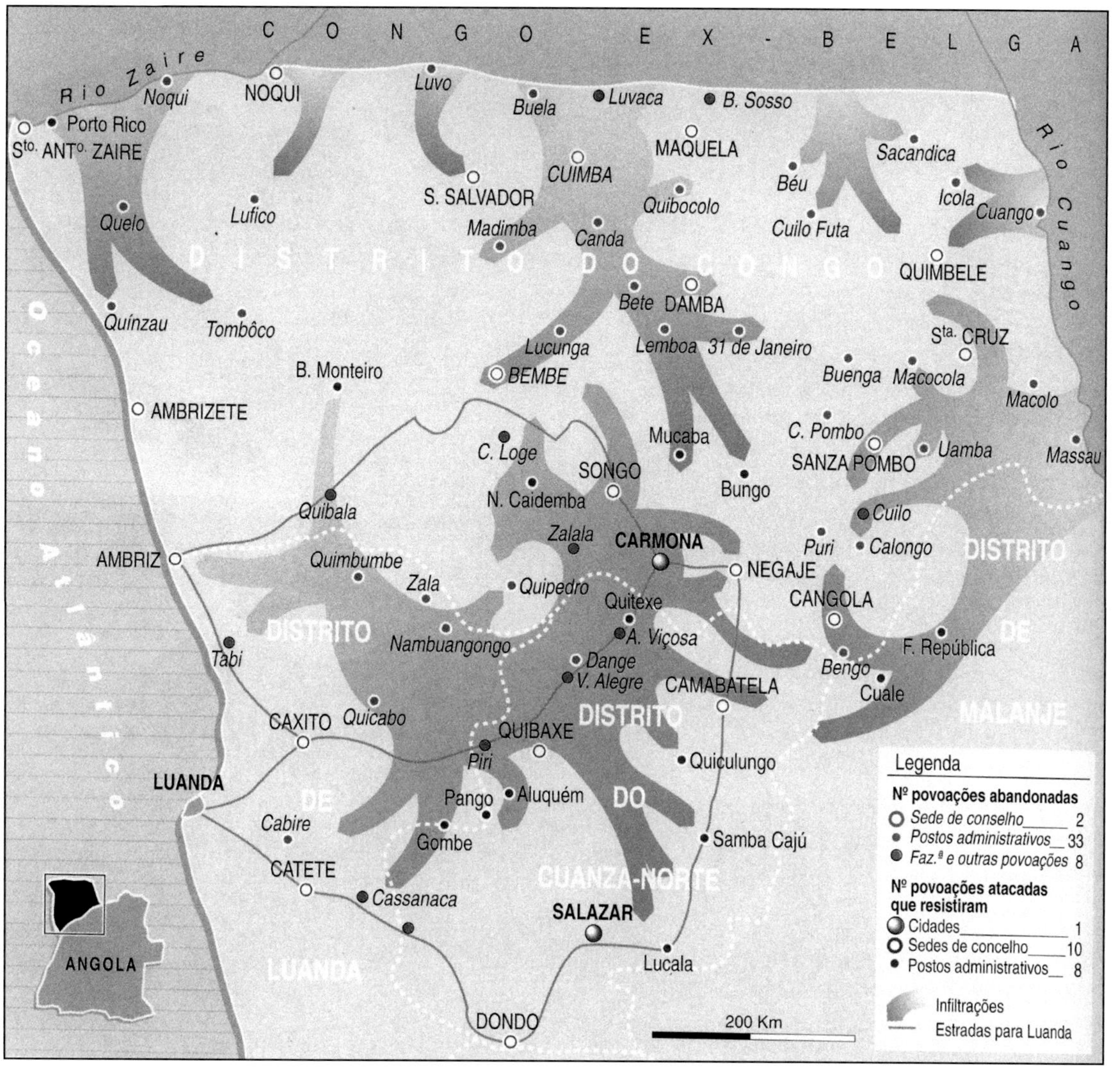

UPA forces in the north of Angola. (*Source Hélio Felgas*)

receipt at UN headquarters in New York. The Brazzaville Delegate announced news of the "revolt," and immediately afterwards, the Liberia Delegate made the motion to condemn Portugal for defending itself and taking measures to restore order.[80]

All of Portugal was shocked at the horror. It has been estimated that 500 Europeans and about 20,000 local people died in this *jacquerie*.[81] The enemy was forced to act against the greater part of the native population that remained faithful to the Portuguese. Moreover, in this assault there were clear acts of intertribal rivalry. The UPA was based on the Bacongo people. In the north on the farms and estates there was a demand for labour to harvest crops, and these jobs were largely filled by Bailundo people from the south of Angola. While UPA forces were initially friendly to the Bailundos, after 7 April, when the enemy began burning the farms as well as the towns of Santa Isabel and Vista Alegre, these migrants began to fight the invaders.[82] As it turned out, the Bailundo workers were intensely loyal, and many died in an attempt to defend themselves, their employers, and Portugal against the Bacongo UPA.[83]

In these initial months, the primary mission of the locally available Portuguese troops was to defend or rescue the threatened population in the three districts of Zaire, Cuanza Norte, and Uíge. This area was roughly the size of continental Portugal and was assigned exclusively to the FAP and its company of Paras, and indeed, the first troops to arrive in the area of Negage were a small detachment of Paras. They established their headquarters next to the Negage runway and their presence gave the population confidence. Soon the Paras took the offensive and began some probing actions, taking their first casualties.

REGIMENT OF PARATROOPS

In May 1961 the Paratroop Regiment (*Regimento de Caçadores Pára-quedistas* or RCP) was authorised, and its headquarters remained at the BCP site in Tancos. It would now oversee four additional battalions in the *ultramar* as well as the support infrastructure of doctors, nurses, chaplains, combat dogs, a command organisation, and the training function that supplied the replacement troops to the battalions. The new battalions were:

- BCP 21, Luanda, Angola, created in May 1961 after the first of its three companies (*companhia de caçadores pára-quedistas* or CCP) were deployed in April.
- BCP 12, Bissalanca, Guiné, created in Ocotber 1966 and composed of three CCPs.
- BCP 31, Beira, Mozambique, created in November 1962 and composed of three CCPs.
- BCP 32, Nacala, Mozambique, created in November 1966 and composed of three CCPs.

As we shall see in subsequent chapters, the Paras distinguished themselves in all three theatres as impressive, effective, and feared airmobile insurgent fighters.

CHAPTER 2
NORTH OF ANGOLA

Following the 15 March attacks, the FAP sought to accomplish two tasks as rapidly as possible. First, it needed to deploy the largest possible number of aircraft, flight and ground personnel, and Paras in the shortest possible time, and second, it needed to acquire an inventory of aircraft adaptable to fighting the new war that it faced. Conventional troops were on their way from the *metrópole* by ocean transport and airlift. Between the months of May and December 1961, troop strength in Angola was augmented from 6,500 to 33,477. These troops landed in Luanda and, as they became available over this eight-month period, moved to subdue the threat from the UPA and regain control in the north of the territory.[1] The transition from a small force aimed at reaction and defence to a large one of reoccupation and neutralisation was gradual and occurred over a period of weeks characterised by the pace of reinforcements in both troops and aircraft arriving from the *metrópole*. The advance of the army and Para columns was accompanied by armed aircraft prepared to intervene when necessary. This fire support occurred alongside airlift evacuations, light logistics support, and reconnaissance, and was complementary to the grand operations of Nambuangongo, Quipedro, Serra de Canda, and Sacandica, all of which will be examined shortly.

MORE DANGEROUS UPA/FNLA

In early January 1962, two scholars of Portuguese Africa, George Houser and John Marcum, were hosted by the UPA/FNLA, which proudly conducted a tour of the north to demonstrate how thoroughly entrenched it was. During their two-week stay, the scholars walked more than two hundred miles over an "interwoven network of trails leading through forests and elephant grass, across vine and single-log bridges, and around open-pit animal traps to the hidden semiportable villages that constituted nationalist Angola."[2] Marcum describes an area apocryphally controlled by the UPA/FNLA that reached from the northern border roughly 200 miles deep into Angola and extended 150 miles in width – an incredulous 30,000 square miles.[3] Within this zone the UPA/FNLA had ostensibly established a rudimentary system of self-government. Ideally everyone travelled with an identity card or *guia* issued by the UPA/FNLA in Léopoldville, and this card was checked frequently, as people travelled the paths and often crossed between one of the fifty UPA/FNLA "administrative districts."[4] The coordinating centre for the UPA/FNLA lines of communication was an encampment known as Fuessi (Portuguese) or Fuesse (French), which was located about halfway between the frontier posts of Luvo and Buela and overseen by the functionary Frederico Deves.[5] From here the trails led south some fifty miles to an operational headquarters near Bembe, where the UPA/FNLA operational commander João Batista received desperately needed weapons and munitions and rationed them to the forty-odd military sectors whose representatives gathered periodically to receive their lot.[6]

Since the March attacks, the UPA/FNLA had continuously received instruction in fighting techniques and material aid, and this external support began to alter the face of the conflict. The *canhangulos*, primitive firearms made with water pipes stolen from farms, were exchanged for automatic rifles. The frontal attacks were replaced with the refinement of ambushes, each more carefully

Diagram of the UPA organisation in the North of Angola.

(Source História das Tropas Pára-Quedistas Portuguesas)

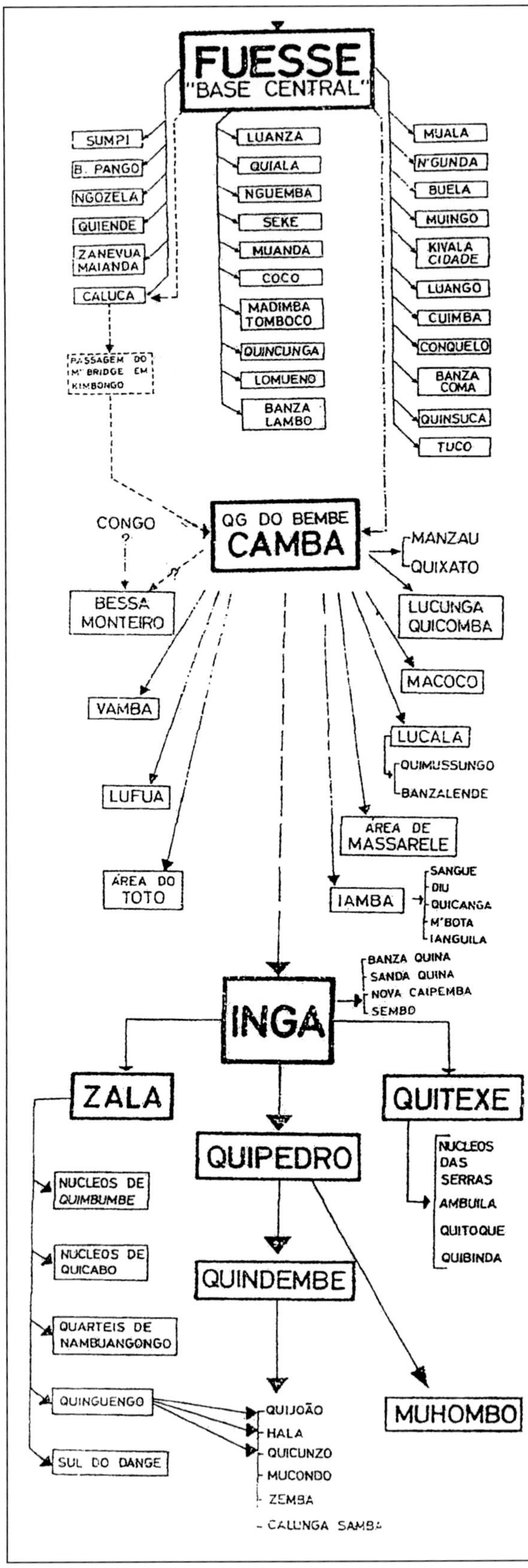

A blank UPA identity card or *guia*. (*Source História das Tropas Pára-Quedistas Portuguesas*)

The T-6 armed trainer was the primary air support aircraft for the "Paras" and other ground forces. (*Source Força Aérea Portuguesa)*

The BCP 21 Coat of Arms, which as a small metal insignia was worn on the left breast pocket of the uniform. (*Source História das Tropas Pára-Quedistas Portuguesas*)

planned, as UPA/FNLA cadres gained experience. Mines began to appear in the main unpaved roads and their dirt trail access routes. As the enemy changed his methods, so did the Portuguese troops.

The war of the guerrilla became increasingly prominent, particularly in the more remote areas away from the commercial and military centres. UPA/FNLA guerrillas destroyed crops and constantly threatened the more remote and isolated farming communities. Occasionally advancing Portuguese troops uncovered arms caches and suffered losses, as pacification gained momentum. Little by little the enemy was driven back.

The first group of fifty-two Paras departed Lisbon on 16 March, arrived in Luanda the next day, and immediately began their march to Carmona to defend the town. The second contingent of two platoons arrived on 19 March, and by the end of the month these several contingents had been organised into the 1st Parachute Company (1CCP). Additional Paras arrived in mid-April and joined the 1CCP to form the Advance Combat Detachment (*Destacamento Avançado de Combate* or DAC). The DAC was lodged in the Fortaleza de São Miguel in Luanda. By the end of April the 2CCP and the 3CCP were formed and added to the force, and on 8 May these companies were combined to form BCP 21. The 1CCP continued to be headquartered in the Fortaleza, while the 2CCP moved to Belo Horizonte next to the Luanda-Catete road, and the 3CCP moved to the "Old Hangar" at the Luanda airbase. The BCP staff also moved into the Fortaleza. In April 1964, BCP 21 purpose-built a new installation at Belas, a village twelve-miles distant from Luanda.

Fortaleza de São Miguel in 1972, initial headquarters of BCP 21 and 1CCP in Luanda. (*Source personal archive of Mário Mendes*)

The purpose-built headquarters of BCP 21 in Belas. (*Source Força Aérea Portuguesa*)

PARANURSES

Following the March 1961 UPA/FNLA assault, Arriaga noted in visiting the hospitals and wounded in Angola that there was a void, an incapacity, in the ability to provide immediate medical care to the wounded and particularly during their evacuation in the field. In exploring this deficiency, he examined the availability of male nurses in the army who might become Paras and soon hit upon the idea that female nurses might better serve the purpose. For conservative Portugal, this notion of putting the gentler sex in harm's way was quite *avant guarde* and required considerable ground work, if it were to be successful.[7] On the positive side, it was easier to introduce new fighting concepts into the FAP, as there was little opposition

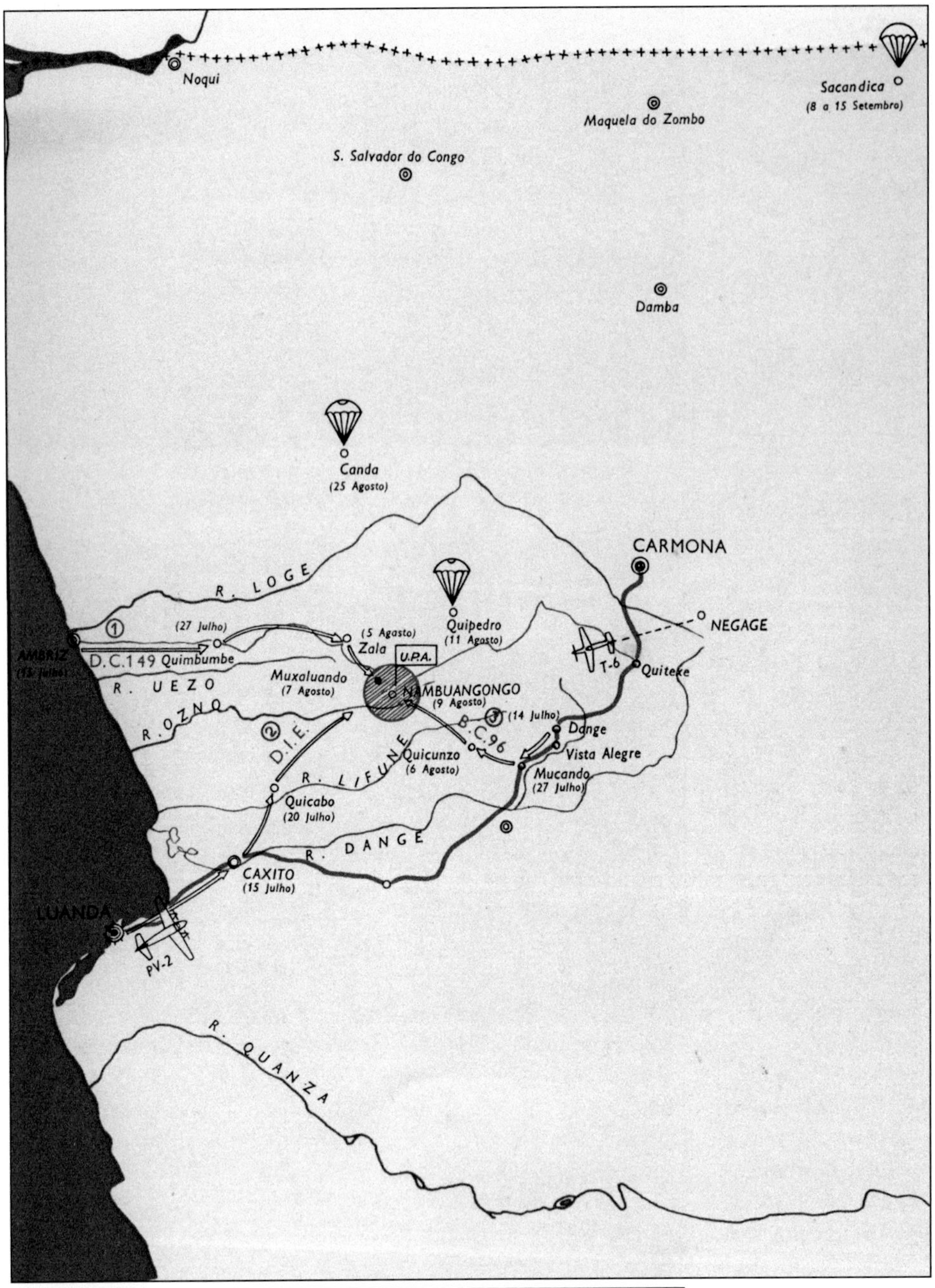

Key Operations in Retaking the North of Angola 1961. (*Source Força Aérea Portuguesa*)

A sister from one of the nursing schools at a training jump for their former nursing students greeting two of the "Six Marias". *Source Força Aérea Portuguesa*)

from any hidebound tradition and consequently little resistance to change. Nevertheless, in socially conservative Portugal, where this concept was a contradiction of the traditional role of women, it had to be cleared at the highest levels of government. Originally Salazar expressed some concerns about the nurses serving in isolated environments surrounded by men; however, Arriaga assured him that all volunteers would be selected from nursing schools run by the Roman Catholic church and would thus be imbued with a strong morality.[8] Indeed the sisters who ran the schools were very supportive of the plan and were invited to award the distinctive green beret to their former students on their graduation from military training.[9] Arriaga accordingly established the Corps of Paratroop Nurses (*Corpo de Enfermeiras Pára-quedistas*) as part of the FAP health system in early 1961, and the first course began on 6 June with five officers and one sergeant, all of whom had the same given name, Maria, and thus became known affectionately as the "six Marias."[10] At the graduation on 8 August following the final of six qualifying jumps, the sisters did indeed award the new paranurses their coveted berets.

In early 1973, the journalist Al Venter interviewed a sergeant paranurse, Maria Natércia de Conceição Pais, who had at the time

Sergeant Natércia Pais on a MEDEVAC mission in early 1973 in Guiné. (*Source personal archive of Al Venter*)

served four years in the Corps, three of which were in Guiné. Previously she had worked as a receptionist in a physician's office and had never been more than fifty kilometres from her village in northern Portugal, where she was born. After graduating from her local school, she felt unchallenged and faced the dreary prospect of marrying a local man and living the remainder of her life in "the confines of a closed, parochial society and eventually dying within a day's walk, perhaps, of where she had been born."[11] When the opportunity presented itself, she promptly enlisted. Altruism apparently played only a small part of her initial motive; however, her subsequent experience in training and field work produced a nurse with drive, personality, and winsomeness. She was now part of a professional team in Guiné whose dozen members led a difficult and often hazardous existence.[12] Her recruitment had been part of a bold step by Portugal in seeking women to ease its manpower shortage and recognising that there are some things a woman can do better than a man, particularly in providing a link between the wounded and normal life outside of combat. During the fourteen years that the program existed there were nine courses graduating a total of forty-eight paranurses, all of whom operated in a combat environment.[13]

NAMBUANGONGO

Nambuango was a thriving small town situated on the western edge of the mountainous Dembos forest about 180 kilometres northeast of Luanda and in the centre of a region rich in coffee cultivation. It was remote enough to be vulnerable to the UPA/FNLA attacks and was savagely assaulted on 16 March. Following the murder of its population of nearly 300 Europeans, the local UPA/FNLA leadership established its headquarters there and for five months rained terror on the surrounding countryside. Because of this successful regional savaging, the UPA/FNLA Cadre Chief Maneca Paca named Nambuangongo the "terrorism capital of Angola." Within the month he would die in an encounter with Special Infantry Battalion 96 (BCE 96).[14]

By the middle of July, Portugal had assembled enough manpower and equipment to launch an offensive against this stronghold and began a three-pronged attack known as Operation VIRIATO.[15] The initial column, which was composed of Cavalry Detachment 149, departed on 15 July from Ambriz, some 154 kilometres from the objective, and proceeded east on the Quimbumbe–Zala route. The second column, composed of an infantry tactical unit reinforced with artillery and engineering components, departed Luanda on the same day and proceeded northeast on the Caxito-Quicabo axis across the Lifune River. The third column, composed of Special Infantry Battalion 96, departed Dange and followed the Vista Alegre–Mucondo (Mucando)–Zemba-Quiraundo (Quicunzo)–Muxaluando route. Throughout the advance of these three columns the FAP provided air cover and reconnaissance with PV-2s from Luanda and T-6s from the Negage airfield in a closely coordinated air-ground support effort.

Once the columns were advancing, FAP aircraft overflew Nambuangongo, or 'Nambu," as the troops called it, and confirmed that it was being abandoned and that UPA/FNLA forces were taking to the bush. This development meant that ambushes from the tall grass bordering the roads and trails would pose the greatest danger. Thus, it became the primary FAP mission to scout ahead and around the advancing ground forces, to alert them to enemy presence, and to destroy any detected UPA/FNLA elements with air attacks. The columns were constantly forced to halt to clear obstacles, and on these occasions the aircraft would provide a protective perimeter. Felled trees lay across the roads, and bridges had been destroyed right down to the foundation piers – all done with explosives stolen from salt mines in the nearby Quicabo region. The PV-2s spent hours and hours manoeuvring over the columns, as they moved through difficult terrain and constant rains. This protective air cover was complemented by supply drops from cargo aircraft between Quicabo and Nambuangongo.[16] Nambuangongo was reclaimed at 1745 on 9 August.

On reflection this had been a complicated and dangerous undertaking with a multi-column force, and there had to be a a better way to avoid the difficult and crippled infrastructure and the ambushes of the UPA/FNLA troops. A leapfrog blow by the Paras was the apparent answer; however, the element of surprise would have to await the arrival of helicopters. In a parachute assault the preliminary activity was obvious to any enemy in the vicinity of the landing zone (LZ), and its observation enabled him to flee and hide or set an ambush. Nevertheless, the speed of advance using an air

Paras jumping over Quipedro, view from the aircraft. (*Source Força Aérea Portuguesa*

Paras jumping from C-54 transport aircraft over Quipedro. *Source Força Aérea Portuguesa*)

assault by the Paras had great advantages at the time over a ground advance, as it increased pressure on the enemy and threw him off balance. Quipedro would be the first such operation.

QUIPEDRO

To increase pressure on the UPA/FNLA and accelerate the advance of Portuguese forces Portugal initiated Operation NEMA to retake the next objective, Quipedro. It began promptly on 11 August following the reoccupation of Nambu. Quipedro was a major UPA/FNLA node serviced by bases running from the Congo through Fuessi, Camba (Bembe), and Inga. For the Paras, this would be the first of only ten jumps during the war between August 1961 and April 1963, and these were undertaken because there were insufficient helicopters at the time for such an assault. Later, when the helicopter squadron was formed in the late summer of 1962, the Paras would increasingly become helicopter-transported air-assault troops. In the meantime, the Para jumps and air-dropped sustainment supplies from the Dornier worked well.

The concept of operations was to have Cavalry Detachment 149 continue its advance through Nambu on the road to Quipedro. The detachment would link up with the 1CCP, which would be dropped into an LZ adjacent to the village. The UPA/FNLA cadres on leaving Nambu had proceeded north in the direction of Bembe and

Paras of the 1CCP readying the makeshift airfield at Quipedro. This was to be used to resupply the Paras by air, but after a Dorner landed and nearly wrecked itself because of the uneven surface, all further resupply missions were air drops. (*Source Força Aérea Portuguesa*)

Caipenda, and thus it was hoped to establish a successful hammer and anvil manoeuvre in which the Paras would land behind the UPA/FNLA and act as a blocking force for the cavalry to drive the rebels into the waiting Paras. PV-2s from Luanda and T-6s from Negage would support both forces.

Early on the morning of the operation there were the traditional briefings for the pilots and Paras to coordinate the drop zone

Aerial view of the village of 31 de Janeiro. (*Source Força Aérea Portuguesa*)

references, markers, and all of the other pertinent technical details. At 1000 hours the C-54s took off from Luanda with the Paras and headed for Quipedro. Thirty minutes before the jump a Dornier marked the objectives to orient the PV-2s and their fire support. The PV-2s and T-6s then covered the vegetation of the LZ, and its surrounds with withering fire to ensure there would be no enemy ambush of the landing Paras. The transports established a right-hand turn pattern over it for the drops, while a Dornier coordinated the operation.[17] The first drop carried the pathfinders who marked the landing zone with fluorescent cloth strips and smoke flares. Next came the Paras and finally the provisions, munitions, and medical supplies.[18] All of this activity gave ample warning to the UPA/FNLA.

After the Paras had landed, regrouped, and moved the 600 metres from the LZ to the village, they remained unchallenged and found a deserted Quipedro. To avoid the suppressing fire and Paras from above, the UPA/FNLA occupants had moved into the nearby ravines that were covered with trees and foliage and thus became invisible and safe from the advancing ground forces and the aircraft circling overhead.[19]

While the Paras met no enemy, the cavalry detachment was not so fortunate. Rather than moving on foot, the detachment was mounted in vehicles and bound to the road bordered by high grass. As the column of vehicles proceeded, it encountered log barriers across the road that had to be cleared. When the column halted to remove the barriers, the detachment found itself in a classic ambush scenario and took intense fire from UPA/FNLA gunmen hiding in the thick, tall grass fifteen to twenty feet high growing right to the edge of the road. It was precisely as the men left the vehicles and were most vulnerable that the rebels attacked. This skilful setting of ambushes and the creation of killing zones were new refinements that clearly came from communist bloc advisors. Rebel ambushes increasingly made good use of the terrain, another newly imported skill. They also had abandoned their home-grown weapons of primitive shotguns and bush knives for modern automatic weapons, and during these attacks wore a quasi-uniform of blue trousers with white or red bands on them.[20] Still despite this new look, UPA/FNLA forces were not military professionals in that they continued their unrestrained acts of savagery and barbarism.

While the reoccupation of Quipedro was successful, the UPA/FNLA was able both to escape the village and the Paras and to lay effective ambushes on the attacking column. The necessary element of surprise was completely absent from Portuguese planning, and the UPA/FNLA made the most of this deficiency. Later with the arrival of helicopters in numbers, this would be corrected.

Likewise at Quipedro the FAP experimented with air supply of its Paras. The extended lines of communication from Luanda, the logistics hub some 245 kilometres distant, made resupply by poor roads tedious and lengthy, and an alternative was needed. The Paras did clear a makeshift landing field near the village and prepared to receive a Dornier. While supplies had been dropped during the operation, it was considered an important capability to be able to land next to the troops to unload fragile cargo that could not survive a drop and evacuate the sick and wounded. On completion of the improvised landing strip, a Dornier nearly wrecked itself in landing because of the uneven surface. While it took off successfully, there would be no more attempts at this field, and only air drops would be used for resupply until the column advanced to a capable and proven site. This experimentation in the use of a Dornier was driven by the lack of helicopters. Ultimately their arrival would change the circumstances, and the Dornier would no longer attempt such risky operations. This pilot survived and was lucky, but it was not always so.

A flight of Noratlas aircraft on their way to an LZ and the dropping of a stick of Paras. *Source Força Aérea Portuguesa*)

Paras of the 2CCP preparing to board their aircraft for the drop into Serra de Canda. The paranurse to the right is Maria Ivine Reis and her colleague to the centre bottom is Maria Arminda. (*Source Força Aérea Portuguesa*)

Members of the 2CCP aboard one of the transport aircraft just prior to the jump into Serra de Canda. (*Source Força Aérea Portuguesa*)

SERRA DE CANDA

Because of the slow and laboured progress overland in retaking Nambuangongo and Quipedro, it was thought that another quick strike from the air would leapfrog the road problems. These were not to be taken lightly. For example, the Baptist missionary David Grenfell noted that between Bungu and 31 de Janeiro, a stretch of about thirty kilometres, the road was blocked by 800 trees and 200 trenches.[21] As there were still inadequate numbers of helicopters available in Angola, a Para drop at Quipedro had been the only viable alternative to advancing quickly. This insertion had worked well in putting troops where they were wanted, and while there were teething problems, the overall success of the operation appeared to merit a repeat. Certainly using the Paras would avoid the trees felled across roads, covered pits dug in the roads, destroyed bridges, mines, and ambushes—each occurring with increasing frequency.

Exactly two weeks after Quipedro, the FAP launched Operation AUTA on 25 August as a clearing operation in the Serra da Canda. Aerial reconnaissance and captured documents indicated that this mountainous region had become a refuge for various armed elements and served as a waypoint for UPA/FNLA cadres coming from the Congo and infiltrating into the areas of Carmona, Toto, Vale do Loge, and Dange.[22]

Canda was a difficult area, as it had a median altitude of 1,000 metres and covered some 1,200 square kilometres. It had the geographic outline similar to the face of a laundry pressing iron with its front pointing south and its rear nearly abutting the Congo frontier. In the west it was defined by the M'Bridge River, and in the east by the meandering Lefunde and its tributaries. The area was particularly difficult to reach during the rainy season when flying weather was irregular with clouds and mist, and the roads often a quagmire.

The concept of operations followed that of Quipedro with the collateral purpose of demonstrating Portuguese capabilities to a larger international audience. After extensive and discrete aerial reconnaissance, an LZ was identified next to the settlements of Pingo and Banza-Tadi located about seventy-five kilometres northeast of Toto in the plain between the Lefunde and M'Bridge Rivers and south of the 1,110-metre peak of Bundiungo. The LZ would be cleared using a large number of incendiary bombs to burn off the grass and facilitate landing by the 2CCP, a force of 120 men divided into four platoons, and its pathfinder team. Once on the ground, the Paras would reconnoitre the surrounding area, set ambushes, advance into the Serra, eliminate the enemy, and join with two army columns, one advancing south from Maquela do Zombo and the other north from Lucunga. The southbound column was composed of a battery of artillery, an infantry company, and a reconnaissance platoon. The northbound column was a forty-man army equipment recovery detachment.

The Paras would all carry the new, light 7.62 calibre ArmaLite AR-10 battle rifle, and their heavier equipment would be left behind to give them added mobility. There also would be two paranurses on five-minute standby at the airfield in Toto with a forward-deployed helicopter to evacuate the wounded.[23]

Four paratroop-capable transport aircraft would be required to effect the drop, and these were three C-54s that came from Lajes Field in the Azores, and from the *metrópole*. The fourth, a Noratlas, was lent by the French from its air base at Pointe Noire, as the Portuguese Noratlases at the time were the civil version without the lateral doors for Para drops. Later the Portuguese Noratlases would be converted for such drop capability.

The enemy was lightly armed, mobile, and avoided the open areas and roadways that would expose him to detection and fire by aerial reconnaissance. He was shy of direct confrontation with superior numbers and firepower and limited his activity to ambushes on isolated forces and proselytising the population. Because of this behaviour, the air staff felt that he would maintain his distance from the Paras in their descent and landing phases, as he would be fleeing the area around the LZ. The risk, therefore, from enemy fire was considered minimal.[24] It was not the desired plan but the one that Portugal could execute with the resources at hand.

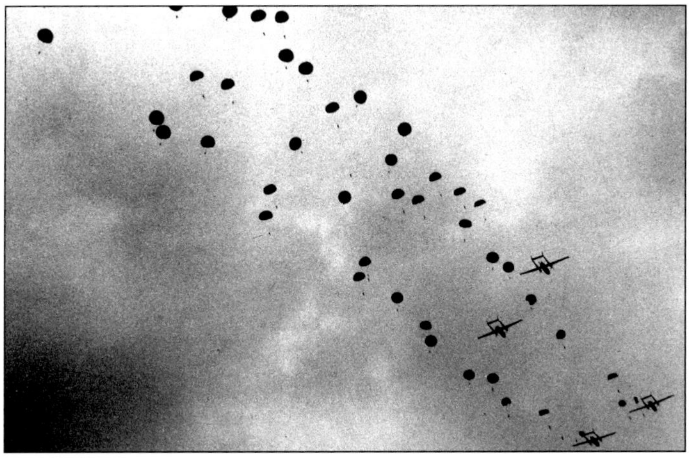

The 2CCP jumping over the Serra de Canda. (*Source Força Aérea Portuguesa*)

Loading a Dornier for a TLCA mission. (*Source Força Aérea Portuguesa*)

Further, the attempted use of the Dornier to replace the helicopter, as at the improvised landing strip at Quipedro, or the dependence for logistics support on a vehicle column making its way to the LZ from Lucunga some fifty kilometres distant were too clumsy and vulnerable to disruption. Again, the day following the jump the Paras prepared a short improvised landing strip next to the LZ in the village of Banza-Tadi, which permitted the landing of light aircraft but again under the most hazardous conditions.[25] Only a single landing was ever effected and that was to bring the commander of the parachute battalion to the LZ. Because of the irregularity of the airstrip and hence safety, further landings were prohibited. Cargo was air dropped into the landing zone as an alternative, but even with reduced speed and altitude there was significant cargo loss from contact with the ground.

These early trials were the beginnings of what was to become an innovative and successful technique of resupply based on the Dornier aircraft and became the mainstay in supplying troops in the field over the remainder of the campaign in the north. Such cargo airdrop missions (*transporte ligeiro de carga aérea* or TLCA) required extraordinary pilot skill and flying precision. The pilot would fly very low and slow, thirty-five to forty knots at full flaps over the objective. The side door of the Dornier was removed prior to the mission, and the mechanic, secured by a harness anchored to the aircraft, pushed twenty-kilogram sacks through the door on the pilot's signal. The sacks were doubled, the inner one containing the goods and the slightly larger, outer one containing the cargo wrapped in a protective padding of elephant grass. The procedure proved successful, and rarely did a sack burst.[26]

The Paras regrouped in the settlement of Pingo, 400 meters south of the LZ, following the jump and found it deserted.[27] The company then split into two detachments of two platoons each to reconnoitre the area. One detachment headed northeast toward Zanza Coma, and the other toward the confluence of the M'Bridge and Lefunde Rivers. Neither detachment made contact with the enemy but did recover documents that revealed the UPA/FNLA organisation in the area. During 26 and 27 August the Paras established ambush sites on the trails and found only three local Bembe natives fleeing the enemy.[28] He had moved from the area to avoid contact with a superior force in classic guerrilla style.

On 28 August, as the company began probing the Serra, it was ambushed but suffered no casualties. It captured five enemy elements and a number of weapons. During the days that followed, clearing operations progressed without enemy contact. Indeed, the population had also fled from the potential conflict and vanished into the sea of elephant grass and dense vegetation. Many crossed the border into the Congo. In the end, the Serra da Canda ceased to be a safe refuge for the UPA/FNLA, at least for the moment

After eight days, the Paras linked with the army column and then returned to Luanda, completing the operation. This type of search and destroy mission highlighted two aspects of specialised troops in counterinsurgency. First, troops with a high level of training and cohesiveness proved very effective in moving against a difficult, dangerous, and evasive enemy. This lesson would lead to the expansion of elite forces in the FAP Paras and navy *fuzileiros* (marines), and establishment of the army commandos.

Second, parachuting a force requires substantial preparation on the ground in readying the LZ, marking it, inserting the pathfinders, and regrouping the forces once on the ground. This activity takes time and thus not only alerts the enemy but also gives him adequate notice to evacuate the area or make other military decisions. Without the element of surprise, it is nearly impossible to damage the enemy in counterinsurgency. In August of 1961, this type of operation was the best of available alternatives, and more effective tactics would await the arrival of helicopters in numbers, the formation of additional elite units, and refinement of tactics.

SACANDICA

Sacandica was a *posto* located twenty-five kilometres south of the Congo frontier and 150 kilometres east of the airfield at Maquela do Zombo. It was overrun in the initial hours of the UPA/FNLA assault on 15 March and had been in enemy hands since then. Because of its distance from the current disposition of land forces, it was assigned to the FAP and its Paras. In planning Operation SARA, the FAP initially believed that a Noratlas operating from Maquela do Zombo could simply land on the grass runway at Sacandica and discharge the Paras and their equipment, but when the Noratlas arrived over Sacandica, it became apparent that the short runway was no longer usable.

Returning to Maquela do Zombo, the Paras lightened their packs and prepared to jump into the target. There was no pathfinder team immediately available, as the original plan did not require one, so pathfinder duties were performed by a lone Dornier that dropped the needed flares to mark the LZ. Following insertion of the platoon, 1,800 kilograms of cargo were dropped. This was enough to last the small force for twenty days, the time thought necessary to complete the mission.[29] The *posto* was held by a strong, fanatical contingent and required some fierce fighting over twenty-nine days, until it was finally freed on 14 October. During this action, the thirty men were resupplied entirely by air.

(Insert nearby Photo 2.17: Paras raising the national flag at the conclusion of Operation SARA in front of the Pousada de Felicidade, the only significant building at the Sacandica *posto*. (*Source Força Aérea Portuguesa)*

BANZA-QUINA

The Paras were next dropped on 14 April 1962over the settlement of Banza-Quina to destroy a major enemy base in the region of Inga just north of the designated LZ in the Vale do Loge. The Vale do Loge was a remote forested valley that followed the Loge River. There were few roads worthy of the name there, although it was crisscrossed with a network of trails that connected settlements and enabled commerce. Coffee was grown by local farmers on the ridges that formed the valley and often these plots were clandestine in order to avoid the tax collector. This illegal practice and the fact that it had to be done remotely made the farmer vulnerable to the insurgents, and they would pressure him to supply them with food, shelter, and perhaps recruits to fight. A farm growing substantial crops over and above a level necessary to feed the farmer's family was certain to be feeding insurgents. Such farms were easily identified by aerial reconnaissance, and this was the case at the settlement of Inga.[30]

Operation SANTO HUBERTO (Saint Hubert), named for the patron saint of hunters, supported the manoeuvre of army units attempting to clear the area of insurgents. The Para force consisted of two groups: the first from the 1CCP and the second from the 2CCP. All total, there were 127 Paras dropped from a Noratlas and two C-54s.[31]

Following the jump, the Paras experienced great difficulty in reorganising in the LZ because it was covered in elephant grass between two and three metres high. Once regrouped, the Paras made their way to Inga, where they discovered an extensive but abandoned enemy base of 150 huts and burnt them to the ground.[32] This concluded the operation.

FUESSI

While Portuguese forces had reoccupied the key centres of the north, they had not eliminated the rebels in the least. UPA/FNLA forces still controlled in various degrees a vast area that ran deep into the north from the Congo border.[33] The conflict had shifted from a fluid chaos into an organised insurgency. UPA/FNLA lines of communication now ran from the Congo over an intricate and constantly changing system of footpaths to Fuessi and continued south some fifty miles into Angola.

UPA/FNLA forces were organised into small "mobile groups" of ten to twelve men suited to hit and run action, of which there were about forty that ranged as far south as Úcua on operations.[34] These groups travelled trails, crossed bridges, and rested in concealed areas. These rest areas had shelters and other infrastructure that represented attractive targets should they be identified by armed aerial reconnaissance.[35] The UPA/FNLA countered this increasingly effective surveillance with slit trenches as air raid shelters, mock villages as decoy targets, and a warning system of spotters. According to Marcum and Houser, the air raids were devastating despite these countermeasures.[36] Fuessi was subsequently dismembered in an operation during the last week of April 1962, three months after Marcum and Houser's visit and Batista's death on 6 February.[37] Portuguese intelligence had identified the dangerous settlement and headquarters, from where mobile groups were regularly laying ambushes throughout the area, and sought to destroy the centre and its ability to make mischief.[38]

On 20 April 1962, the 1CCP was airlifted from Luanda to Sao Sãlvador and began its operation to neutralise Fuessi. The objective was about thirty kilometres to the east of Luvo in an area that was difficult to access. The only route was by a footpath that had not been travelled in a year and was thought to be abandoned. The company of 120 men travelled by truck from São Salvador to Mamarrosa and after that followed a road next to the River Gunguege until reaching the River Lunguege. Here the troops forded and proceeded on foot, as the bridge had been destroyed, and the vehicles could not continue. The rough roadway leading away from the bridge degenerated into a path that was overgrown and difficult to follow. It was also crossed by others, and the route became very confusing. The guide, Pedro Tumissongo, was familiar with the routes around Luvo and south, but the company had left the area that he knew, and now it depended on a Dornier from Negage to provide orientation and to drop supplies, as the troops travelled with light packs for mobility.[39] This help and the size of the force would have made enough of a disturbance to destroy any element of surprise, as UPA/FNLA lookouts and sentries could hear and see the aircraft and detect the approaching column. It was the rainy season, and the heat and humidity made going difficult, even travelling with light loads. The progress was further impeded by the need to be on guard against ambushes, although it was likely that the presence of the Dornier forewarned the insurgents and caused them to retire. Still, there were four additional rivers and miles of bush to cross before arriving at Fuessi, and the pace was labored.

The company reached the Rivers Mata-Matende, Cai, and Magina and forded them before finally reaching the Luvo, which was wide and swollen by the rains and had a swift, powerful current. It took time to rig a line and to cross carefully, one by one, but it was done without incident, and the march resumed at an accelerated pace. The company reached Fuessi at noon and quietly deployed, encircling

Paras of the 1CCP rigging a line across the Luvo River, which was wide and swollen by rains. Its current was swift and powerful and presented a time-consuming obstacle. (*Source Força Aérea Portuguesa*)

Paras of the 1CCP await a supply drop over the abandoned UPA/FNLA headquarters at Fuessi, April 1962. (*Source Força Aérea Portuguesa*)

the compound and establishing a counter-ambush formation. Even so, UPA/FNLA lookouts would have been alerted by the Dornier and the approaching paratroops. When the Paras entered the compound, it was deserted, but there were warm fires, food, plates and utensils, and other abandoned property. There were even photographs of "mademoiselles" with inscriptions written across them in French and local idioms.[40] In the largest hut, which housed the insurgent leaders, there was a notice posted on an exterior wall. Pedro Tumissongo read it for the Paras: "It is easy to enter into this place but difficult to leave; blacks who enter must obey, thereafter, the orders of Holden Roberto."[41] The disappointment was extreme for the Paras, but then this failure held lessons that would lead to more effective operations. Guides would become more competent; force sizes, reduced; and power projection, more comfortable with the bush. Dorniers alerting the enemy would become a thing of the past.

QUIPEDRO

The Paras remained active, and on 16 August 1962 in Operation BARRETE VERDE (Green Beret) the 2CCP jumped into an LZ at Quipedro with 116 men in an operational training mission. It was the fifth jump by the Paras, and their unpredicted presence at this key node in the enemy infrastructure kept him off balance.[42]

INGA AND BANZA-QUINA

Operation FURRIEL DANTAS (Quartermaster Dantas), the Paras' sixth jump, was conducted two months later on 3 October in the Vale do Loge with the jump of a two-platoon detachment, one platoon from the 1CCP and the other from the 2CCP – a total of eighty-five men, all launched from a Noratlas. The operation was prompted by the identification through aerial reconnaissance of several enemy bases in the valley and the need for their destruction. The attack began the evening before with the aerial bombardment of the camps which alerted the insurgents. When the Paras arrived overhead early the next day for their sixth jump, most of the enemy had fled. The Paras were dropped over the LZ, regrouped on the ground within ten minutes, and quickly moved to their objective. As they encountered fire from the first hut of the enemy base, they returned it and killed five insurgents. The Paras were subsequently to link with a supporting ground force of twelve teams of four men each that would be inserted by helicopter with the objective of sealing the exits to the valley and thus any escape routes. Unfortunately one of the helicopters had mechanical problems, so initially there were only eight teams in the assault. These eight linked with the Paras, and this combined force found numerous abandoned enemy bases, burned hundreds of huts, killed an additional insurgent and captured two women.[43]

The lesson from this operation was that a drop of Paras gave the enemy ample warning while a helicopter assault offered little and was consequently far more effective. The helicopter would soon come into its own and be the preferred assault vehicle in the war.

MAGINA (CALUCA)

A fortnight later on 18 October the 1CCP and 3CCP assaulted the enemy's "Quartel Central" of Caluca in a strike styled Operation PARFUSO GRANDE (Large Vice), the Paras' seventh drop. The enemy base was located in a remote highlands south of São Salvador and just north of the M'Bridge River. Portuguese military planners knew that the base was strongly protected and that the enemy maintained an extensive vigilance through a warning system that extended in a radius measured in dozens of kilometres.[44] Just as earlier Para operations against known enemy bases sought to dismantle the insurgents' infiltration network, this too was aimed to clear a specific area around the base of Caluca, where there was an identified node serviced by Fuessi. Located at the edge of the Mata do Dimba, the second largest virgin forest in Angola, the area was isolated – the perfect safe haven for insurgents to organise themselves, regroup from operations, rearm, and remain unmolested. Consequently the only feasible way to assault the base successfully was to mount a quick and devastating surprise attack with an airborne strike.

The mission was executed in three phases: The first was an attack on Caluca with a heliborne Para detachment for shock. Because there were only four Alouette II helicopters available at the time, the detachment was limited to sixteen and was potentially vulnerable because of its size. This small force was to be quickly reinforced in a second phase by the near simultaneous drop of the 1CCP in an LZ three kilometres distant. The third phase was the subsequent drop of the 3CCP at the same LZ, and its duties were to perform sweeps along the north (right) bank of the M'Bridge River.[45]

By 1000 hours on the 18th weather conditions permitted the

operation to begin, and the first aircraft launched. Air bombardment of the LZ and its surrounds preceded the air assault. At 1149 hours the helicopters arrived and began their hovers over the designated LZ with its unanticipated shrub trees and tall grass, necessitating a jump of three metres to the ground for the Paras. Shortly thereafter the enemy began to flee his base, which the Paras found to be a well camouflaged group of six to eight huts constructed from and covered with the same local vegetation that grew naturally around the base. These had been difficult to identify by aerial observation. The detachment encountered and killed two insurgents. At 1155 hours the 1CCP jumped into its LZ and closed on the objective. At 1355 the 3CCP jumped into the same LZ, began its sweeps of the M'Bridge riverbank, discovered a river crossing, and destroyed the raft associated with it. A company of marines supported this effort and established ambush sites along the riverbank. Three Paras were lightly wounded in the operation and were evacuated by helicopter. Overall twenty-nine of the enemy were killed and five captured. The enemy base at Caluca was destroyed, and this lifted a burden from the local population that had been forced to hide in the dense grass and forest.[46]

This initial experience with helicopter assault revealed the potential it had over both parachute jumps and land approaches. It could surprise the enemy and make him vulnerable to small detachments of elite troops placed judiciously, quickly, and suddenly to capture or eliminate him. This was the wave of the future, and its success at Caluca was a forerunner.

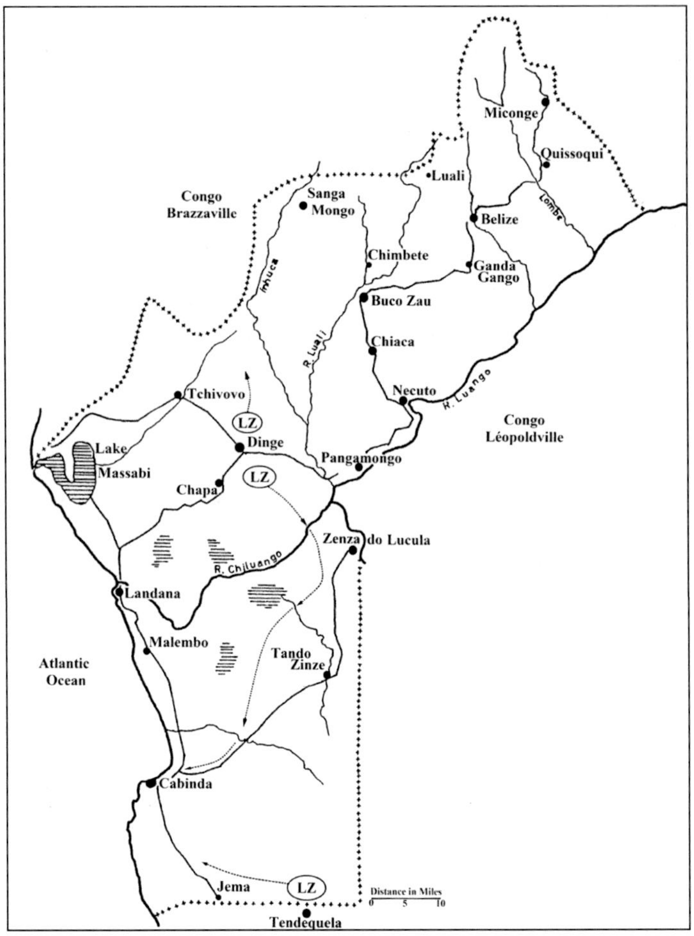

Map of the Cabinda enclave showing Para operations. (*Source the author*)

CABINDA

The final three jumps for the Paras in the Angolan theatre occurred in the enclave of Cabinda. The first, Operation PICA-PAU (Woodpecker), was a jump of the 1CCP on 11 September 1963 into an LZ near the village of Dinge and a subsequent sweep southward by way of the villages of Zenza do Lucula and Tando Zinze along the border with Congo-Léopoldville. The ultimate destination of the operation was Cabinda, the capital. Near Tando Zinze the fourth vehicle in the column hit an antivehicle mine and two Paras were wounded. This was the Paras' first experience with mines, and there were to be many more.[47]

The second, Operation CAÇÁ-LO VIVO (Hot Pursuit) was a jump of the 2CCP over Dinge and the execution of a strike against an enemy encampment on the border with Congo-Brazzaville. The third and last jump was psychological operation designed to send a message to the enemy by having two platoons drop into a zone next to the Congo-Léopoldville border village of Tendequela (Tendequelle). After a sweep of the border, the Paras made their way to Cabinda.[48]

Paras in vehicles on the Zenza-Camame "road". Note the elephant grass growing right to the margins of the trail and providing the enemy cover for ambush. (*Source Força Aérea Portuguesa*)

The Paras were not confined to air insertion and participated in nearly one hundred ground operations against the enemy in the north in the three years between April 1961 and April 1964. With the arrival of the Alouette III, however, tactics changed, and while parachute qualification continued to be the defining centrepiece of training in the *metrópole*, the helicopter replaced it in practice in the *ultramar*.

ARRIVAL OF THE HELICOPTER

During 1958, Portugal acquired seven Sud-Aviation Alouette II helicopters, which represented the initial step in creating an effective helicopter force. The first Alouette II was wrecked in January 1960; however, the remaining six were sent to Angola at the end of 1962 and later, with the acquisition of twelve Alouette III helicopters in the spring and summer of 1963, formed the basis for Squadron 94, the *Moscas* or "Flies," at Luanda. This addition of the helicopter fleet to the resources in Angola had a transformative effect on the war in the development of tactics for initially moving Paras and ultimately all light infantry forces and supporting them with localised firepower.

Depositing troops exactly where they were desired was difficult with a parachute insertion, as there were so many variables and vulnerabilities. The wind was an enormous factor, as it could cause injuries on landing or even cause a miss of the LZ. The LZ may also be some distance from the objective, enabling an alerted enemy to flee or subjecting the LZ to ambush. On the other hand, the helicopter could deposit a force precisely next to an objective for its

Aircrewman manning the helicopter gunship cannon. (*Source Força Aérea Portuguesa*)

Dornier aircraft with its 37mm rocket canisters being loaded. (*Source Força Aérea Portuguesa*)

taking or destruction.[49] It was the perfect answer to mobility in the difficult terrain of the *ultramar*, and illustratively, a one-minute flight in a helicopter equalled about an hour on foot in the African jungle, forests, and grasslands. It was a constant challenge to make contact with the enemy. When contact was made, complete reconnaissance was often impossible or the opportunity for engagement would be lost. Consequently, the Paras required speed, mobility, and flexibility to capitalise on these infrequent opportunities, and the helicopter was the answer to profiting from these and gaining tactical successes.

Initially, the helicopter assault concept was built around the twenty-man combat group. A flight of five helicopters would insert five four-man sections on the ground quickly and judiciously to make the most of insurgent contact. If the flight was expected to encounter resistance and needed covering fire to protect it, then a helicopter gunship or *heli-canhão* with its 20mm cannon covered the insertion and recovery and provided support as required. The development of this gunship capability took several years and was done in consultations with Sud-Aviation.

The key to inserting the Para combat group lay with the lead pilot in the flight. He was invariably an aviator qualified in both helicopters and fixed-wing aircraft, and would spend much of his initial familiarisation flying in the theatre at low altitude in a Dornier over his assigned tactical area. In addition to learning the terrain, he would mark a map with suitable helicopter landing sites that he might use in future operations. In designating the landing sites, he would also mark approach routes to each. These were chosen for their natural terrain features that would mask the arrival of five noisy helicopters and potentially deliver some potential for surprise. Alongside the pilot's area familiarisation, Paras rehearsed operations as a team until the unit was proficient.[50]

Once prepared, the combat group was kept on alert at a primary base, such as Luanda, next to BCP 21 headquarters, until an operation was imminent. At that point the group would relocate to an airfield in the area of anticipated operations, where there might be a wait of several days before an opportunity occurred. The entire success or failure of the mission depended on surprise, and considerable pains were taken to achieve it. Reconnaissance of the target was kept to an absolute minimum to avoid flushing the insurgents prematurely, and discussion of the mission was forbidden outside the secure briefing area.

Once called, the combat group would be given its final briefing and then promptly launched, taking the most direct of several preselected routes to the target and its prescribed LZ.[51] Travelling with the troop transport helicopters in their nap of the earth

A flight of Alouette III troop carriers. (*Source Força Aérea Portuguesa*)

approach, the helicopter gunship would circle and clear the LZ prior to landing the combat group. It would continue to cover the area with its cannon to provide suppressing fire, if required, while the troop carriers were most vulnerable in debarking the assault force. The gunship was much feared by the enemy; however, for additional support there might be a Dornier with two nine-rocket canisters, one under each wing, loaded with versatile French 37mm rockets. They were used either for marking targets with smoke or making an attack on guerrilla sites. After depositing the combat group, the troop carriers would take off and loiter nearby awaiting conclusion of the action, which would generally last only about ten minutes. At its conclusion, the helicopters would land at the nearest suitable site, as the original may or may not be near the concluding action, and load the assault team and perhaps a highly valued prisoner. The team would then be airlifted to another objective.

The Para combat group with its helicopter transport would normally remain in the field throughout the day, pursuing the insurgents and coordinating operations with other ground forces. At the conclusion of daylight operations, the combat group would rendezvous with a preselected, specially equipped ground unit with whom to bivouac for the evening. As only select units were equipped with the necessary helicopter field support in fuel, ammunition, and maintenance capability to host an air assault team, this choice required some considerable planning and coordination. During the evening the helicopters would be fuelled and rearmed, and the men rested for further operations the following day. This process continued for three to four days before all returned to the original base.[52]

Upon occasion two air assault teams would be employed

together, thereby doubling the force on the ground from twenty to forty troops. Unless the team was part of a larger operation and formed one of the closing forces in a "hammer and anvil" tactic or a similar manoeuvre, there was a risk that such a small body could be overrun by a larger insurgent force. Thus care had to be exercised not to insert a team into an untenable situation. On the other hand, use of armed helicopters was carefully controlled, so that any damage or casualties in the population were avoided through the overenthusiastic or indiscriminate use of firepower. Helicopter assault operations were always executed away from populated areas.[53] Indeed, the helicopter and its effective utilisation was without question the biggest difference in military capability between that of Portuguese forces and the enemy.

NEW FRONTS

By the mid-1960s, neither the MPLA nor the UPA/FNLA had met with any substantial success in a classic subversion of the population in the north or in truly displacing the Portuguese position there. This lack of insurgent progress occurred for several reasons. While the military lacked both the manpower and mobility to seal the land border completely in an area of poor roads, dissention between the MPLA and the UPA/FNLA, Léopoldville's favouritism of the UPA/FNLA, and Holden Roberto's failure of leadership served to limit any insurgent offensive.[54] Léopoldville's favouritism of the UPA/FNLA was unabashed, and it worked to give its chosen movement every advantage. As an example, Léopoldville because of its own security problems did not permit insurgents to bear arms within its borders. Both the MPLA and UPA/FNLA insurgents would be transported by Congolese soldiers to the Angolan border, where they would be issued their weapons from depositories. On returning from operations, their weapons would be cantoned, and they would return to their training base with a Congolese escort.[55] Léopoldville actually employed this control measure to discriminate against and harass the MPLA. In 1962 the MPLA was often impeded from reaching the border, and its arms confiscated, whereas the UPA/FNLA was accorded privileged and unimpeded access. Despite this among many other advantages, Roberto proved unable to lead effectively in either the political or the military dimension, and Léopoldville sponsorship was unable to reverse this trend.

From the beginning the MPLA had been unwelcome in Léopoldville, and finally in June 1963 moved its headquarters to Brazzaville. Its ability to project itself militarily into Angola became almost completely circumscribed by November, and it looked more and more isolated. In January 1964 at its Conference of Cadres (*Conferencia de Quadros*) in Brazzaville, it was decided to begin rebuilding the movement as a serious revolutionary force. Part of this plan involved opening a front in the east of Angola through Zambia. The MPLA had made overtures to Kenneth Kaunda, the first president of Zambia following its independence from Britain in 1964. It had also befriended Julius Nyerere, the first president of Tanzania, likewise following its independence from Britain in 1962. These relationships were to prove fortuitous. Beginning in 1965, Tanzania and Zambia permitted the transit of Chinese and Soviet weapons and MPLA cadres across their territories to the Angolan border. Because of this access, the MPLA was able to open a major offensive and to conduct an intensive insurgent campaign in the eastern Angolan districts of Moxico and Cuando Cubango. Preparations were begun accordingly, and by the opening months of 1966 proselytising of the population in the east was evident. The first armed incursions occurred in April, and the war had now clearly moved to the east. Portuguese resources were redirected in response to the new threat, but before moving eastward, we need to examine developments in Guiné and Mozambique.

CHAPTER 3
GUINÉ

The platoon of Paras that arrived in Guiné in July 1963 faced a difficult task. The territory was a complicated land in which to project force, and it was thus not easy to secure it against threats from either within or abroad. Its climate was unappealing and hostile. Its topography and geography were difficult, and its population highly fragmented and unevenly distributed. Its economy was built on subsistence agriculture and thus devoid of any reasonable economic potential. In summary, its viability as a Portuguese colony was fragile, and its defence against an insurgency with inviolate sanctuaries nestled immediately opposite its frontiers and from which a resourceful enemy could project its own power proved a supreme challenge.

A COMPLICATED THEATER

Guiné, located in West Africa and sandwiched between Senegal to the north and the Republic of Guinea to the east and south, represented a complicated problem for Portugal for several reasons. First, the country was tropical. The intense humidity and enervating heat made for an oppressive atmosphere. José de Moura Calheiros, a young Para officer, notes that the image of Africa in the *metrópole* was very different from the reality. On exiting his aircraft at Bissalanca, he felt an invisible wave of suffocating heat wash over him, and seconds later to his amazement he was soaked in sweat.[1] While there is a dry season that provides some relief from November to May, it too is not without discomfort. As it nears its end in the late spring months, the sun approaches its seasonal zenith over the territory, and tropical weather systems develop. These are characterised by low pressure areas and strong ascending warm air currents. These updrafts are fed from the continental air mass over the Sahara and create what is termed locally as the "east wind." The population experiences it as a hot, dry airstream that comes from the desert to the east, absorbs moisture from the soil and vegetation, and carries a fine dust that affects those with respiratory problems. This is accompanied by temperatures rising to 100°F (38°C) on average.

The rainy season runs from June to October and ensures a high humidity. It is characterised by frequent monsoons that develop from the disequilibrium between the oceanic and continental air masses. These storms are magnified by the shock of the "east wind," and are characterised by violent electrical activity with the attendant thunder and lightning, tornados, strong winds reaching sixty knots, and heavy rainfall. In the coastal region annual rainfall averages 3.00 meters, and in the interior, 1.25 meters.[2]

Second, the topography of Guiné is difficult. It can be divided roughly into two distinct geographical areas, the north and east (interior) and the west (littoral). The land rises in the northern and eastern interior areas, where the coastal growth gradually disappears, and the terrain becomes forested, as it transitions into the sub-Saharan savanna plain of grasslands and scattered, scrawny trees. Elevation never exceeds 300 meters.[3] The most important, however, is the western one, which on a tactical level is characterised by a forbidding and inhospitable stretch of mangrove and swamp forests covering the coastal inlets and deltas of half a dozen very broad rivers. Tidal action floods twice daily, and as the water rises, it fills these estuaries and creates vast tracts of impenetrable swamp.[4] The banks of these sinuous waterways are mantled with dense, luxuriant vegetation projecting over the water, a condition that is ripe for the ambush of any vessel. Currents in the rivers during flooding and ebbing can reach seven knots, enough to overwhelm the small engines in the majority of river transport. At low tide vast expanses of dreary mud flats (*bolanhas*) are exposed and impede the projection of military power and commerce through the river system. Paras had to cross these rivers and mud flats to engage any enemy, and this entailed either travelling long distances overland by truck, boarding a naval landing craft, or accepting a lift by helicopter. Each method had its limitations. In the case of the roads, they were often poor and impassably flooded in the rainy season and were frequently mined as part of an enemy ambush. Indeed, many of the roads during the rainy season become rivers themselves, making passage all but impossible. The noise of trucks easily alerted the insurgents. Landing craft readily moved the needed volume of forces but, like land travel, were noisy and vulnerable to ambush. Movement by helicopter was rapid, but the limited space available meant that only a small force could be airlifted even with several rotorcraft, and these too were noisy. In short, there was no ideal way to improve on the friction of moving troops.

Third, Guinean geography also played an important role. Officially Guiné has a land area of 36,125 square kilometres, but its twice daily inundation covers as much as twenty-two percent of the country, and reduces the surface area to an estimated 28,000 square kilometres. From this figure an additional 3,200 square kilometres can be deducted for the area periodically flooded by rainwater.[5] Under these considerations, the habitable land mass is about 24,800 square kilometres, or about the size of Switzerland.[6] Its land frontier is about 680 kilometres, of which 300 comprise the northern border with Senegal, and 380 the eastern and southern borders with the Republic of Guinea.[7] Guiné was thus so small that the entire country became essentially a frontier and battle zone, making it extremely difficult to defend. Perhaps the best characteristic of this small area was that there was no part of it that could not be reached by helicopter in thirty minutes.[8]

As if these impediments of climate, terrain, and geography were not enough of a challenge, the population represented a fourth obstacle as much for the insurgents as for the Portuguese. In 1960 the population was 525,437, and was concentrated in the western coastal delta with about one hundred people per square kilometre.[9] The arid eastern half was virtually empty with about one person per square kilometre, and it was here that insurgent infiltration occurred with the least opposition. Over ninety-nine percent of the population was black and fragmented into two primary groupings covering twenty-eight ethno-linguistic groups, each exhibiting various degrees of loyalty either to Portugal or the insurgents. Indicative of early exposure to the Portuguese, the coastal population was Christian or animist. The interior peoples were Muslim, reflecting their contact with the ancient interior trade routes from the Gulf of Guinea through Timbuktu to The Maghreb. Because Guiné was an economic backwater, it was never a country of European colonisation, and there were less than 3,000 whites in the colony.[10]

Defence of this territory was consequently difficult under the best of circumstances. The enemy did not have far to travel from his sanctuaries in Senegal and the Republic of Guinea to reach population centres. With such a short logistics tail that led over only partially challenged waterways and land corridors from the south, and overland routes in remote areas in the north and east, insurgent troops operated in concentrations almost anywhere in the territory. The Portuguese consequently found themselves in a defensive position, where Bissau, the capital and main port and city, was the centre through which all power flowed to support the interior line represented by the frontier or border areas. Because the nature of the battlefield characterised the height of Clausewitzian friction, the absolute key to Para mobility was the helicopter. It would move troops to battle, support them in their fight, and bring them home afterwards.

The initial military offensive begun in 1963 was successful as far as it went; however, it had its limitations for a number of reasons. Initially leadership of the war was divided between Brigadier Fernando Louro de Sousa, the commander-in-chief, and *Comandante* Vasco da Gama Rodrigues, the governor general. While Rodrigues, a naval officer, was a forthright individual with a wealth of operational experience, Louro de Sousa was a staff officer with little practical experience in the field. Because of these two contrasting perspectives, the men clashed constantly, and the campaign against the PAIGC suffered accordingly. Rodrigues attempted to be practical, and Louro de Sousa clung to his theories of conventional war.[11] This division of leadership created a fragmented approach that could not address the war effectively or successfully. It was soon replaced with a new leader and a consolidation of the two offices.

Brigadier Arnaldo Schultz, the Commander-in-Chief and Governor General during the period 1964 to 1968, struck a defensive posture and sought to counterattack the PAIGC as it advanced in an attempt to regain control of lost areas. This strategy was doomed to failure, as it allowed the PAIGC a toehold within national territory and a relatively free hand with the population. Schultz did not see the population as a primary battleground, and while the PAIGC was establishing medical clinics, schools, village markets, and the like, Schultz ignored this enemy proselytization. In fact, it was a key factor in the equation. Schultz pursued a military solution, indeed gambled on it, and the strategy ultimately proved a failure. The small territory was increasingly being overrun and controlled by the PAIGC in the face of his offensives. Early on the PAIGC was able to extend its influence into the northern and southern areas and deep into the east of Guiné in the *chão manjaco* (Manjaco ground). In 1965 it had begun to receive substantial military support from the communist bloc. The momentum was in its favour.

THE PARAS

The initial duties of this Para platoon of one officer, four sergeants, and thirty-five troopers was the security of the air base at Bissalanca, designated initially as AB 2, on the outskirts of Bissau under Operation CORISCO (Lightening). Bissalanca was the principal installation of the Air Force, and these Paras together with a small contingent of air police formed the Mixed Detachment for Immediate Defence of AB 2. As the situation around AB 2 stabilised, the Paras, now known as Platoon No. 111 in the Mixed Detachment, joined with

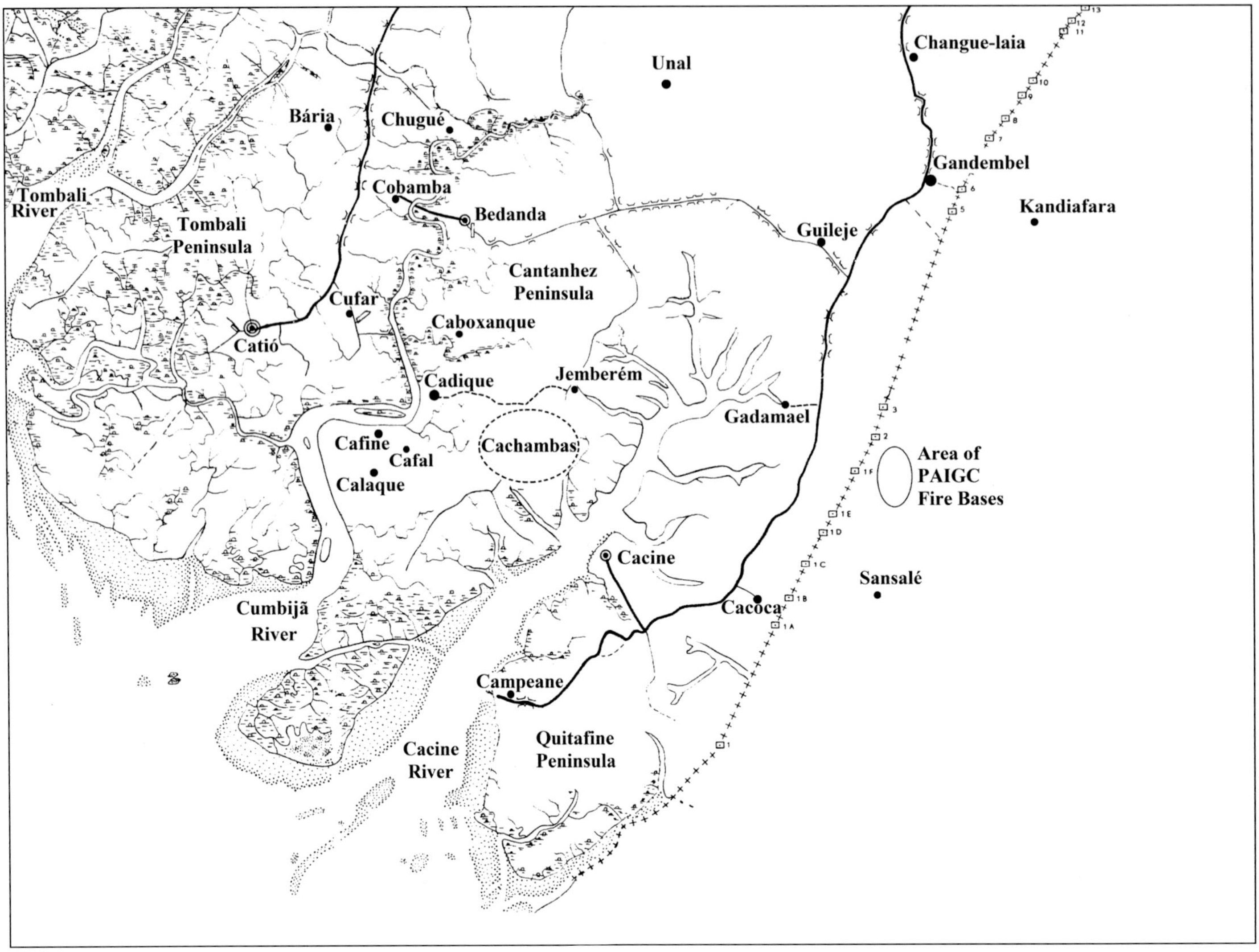

Tombali, Cantanhez and the Quitafine Peninsulas. (*Source the author*)

naval units in August to pursue the PAIGC enemy in Operation ESQUILO (Squirrel). In September there was a proficiency jump over the airfield of the small group. Later in the year the Mixed Detachment was reinforced with a team of war dogs and their handlers.[12] In February 1964 in the area of Cachide on the Island of Como, the Paras suffered their first casualty, Daniel Rosa Neto.[13]

In December the Mixed Detachment led by Captain Luís Tinoco de Faria was reorganised as the Squadron of Land Defence, and in April 1966, he led one of its platoons in an eye-opening Operation GRIFO (Griffon) in the south of Guiné – the focus of the Paras throughout the conflict. PAIGC insurgents from the beginning had showed an elevated preparation for combat, and this was certainly the experience of the Paras that month when they faced a PAIGC unit attempting to enter Guiné through the "Corridor of Guileje." This "corridor" was the favoured entry point and avenue from the Republic of Guinea, as it was opposite the PAIGC base of Kandiafara and provided a direct route inland to the small port town of Bedanda and the interior beyond. The job of the Paras in this case was to establish an ambush along the insurgent route in an attempt to foreclose PAIGC penetration. This they did in the pre-dawn twilight, establishing themselves in key concealed positions to create a "zone of death" with their crossfire and to await the enemy. At about ten o'clock in the morning a group of insurgents appeared and began to move into the kill zone. The PAIGC fighters suddenly sensed they were in danger, as they detected the Paras and fired some passing rounds in the hope of gaining time to withdraw. As the enemy withdrew, the Paras opened fire and caused some losses.[14]

Now, however, the insurgents rapidly executed a counter-ambush movement and brought the Paras under fire from their flank. One of the three insurgents who had survived the kill zone encounter opened fire and hit Tinco de Faria, who was attempting to reorient his men to counter the enemy move. Soon the captain was hit a second time and gravely wounded. In the exchange three insurgents were killed, but the enemy now positioned a heavy machinegun in the cover of the dense grass and began to rake the Para position. During a reloading pause, the Paras attempted to transport their wounded to a position suitable for evacuation. The enemy then changed his tactics and pursued the Paras, raking them with fire from a safe distance. When the Paras arrived at the evacuation site on edge of the River Tenhege and assumed a defensive formation, they suffered new attacks from the shelter of the grass. Eventually the PAIGC moved away, but unfortunately the captain's condition deteriorated, and he died about midday before vital help could reach him.[15] Posthumously he was awarded the Cruz de Guerra, first class, for his actions.[16] This experience clearly sensitised the Paras to the level of enemy skill and violence to be expected in future engagements. Normally insurgents "shoot and scoot," but not the PAIGC. They proved very aggressive and rarely shied from a fight.

In October 1966, BCP 12 was created on paper and activated two months later. It was constituted initially with three companies: CCP 121, CCP 122, and a personnel company. As the conflict intensified, a fourth company, CCP 123, was added in July 1970. At the same

Coat of Arms of Parachute Battalion 12. (*Source Museu das Tropas Pára-quedistas*)

time the BCP established its administrative, logistics, intelligence, and operations sections to support the companies. In December it arrived in Bissau, and the Para platoon there was absorbed into it. The Paras now became an intervention force and reserve and withdrew from the Squadron of Land Defence; however, they still belonged to the FAP, and it faced a major problem in the south.[17]

OPERATION BARRACUDA

The PAIGC had been building its air defence infrastructure on the Cantanhez peninsula to protect its dominance there, and the FAP challenged it in several operations to eliminate this threat and occupation. With its new Para force now available, it was time to conduct an aerial bombing with a follow-on ground force assault to destroy the enemy air umbrella entirely. Earlier purely air operations had at first glance appeared successful; however, the enemy was so thoroughly entrenched with his encampments and their a vast infrastructure of crop cultivation, field hospitals, arms magazines, and living quarters, all beneath a vast complex of powerful antiaircraft artillery, that it was impossible for air power alone to eject him. His antiaircraft defence became increasingly dangerous, as its capability and armament became heavier. These weapons were protected by extensive sand earthworks and positioned tactically to provide mutual protection with interlocking fields of fire while defending PAIGC installations. The gunners were well-disciplined and unusually warlike, uncharacteristic traits for the typical insurgent army. This sophisticated antiaircraft organisation could only have been achieved with the help of outside advisors. At various times these were Soviet, Chinese, or Cuban, and on occasion their bodies would be discovered by ground troops following an air raid.[18] It was clear by now that a follow-up by ground troops was needed after an air attack.

Before going to Cantanhez, however, the new Para companies were tested on a more straightforward operation near their base in Bissalanca. In January 1967, Operation BARRACUDA was planned to capture intact one of the PAIGC antiaircraft guns. There was a particular site opposite Bissau and a short distance upstream on the Geba River near the village of Gã Formoso. It threatened aircraft in the traffic pattern at Bissalanca and could not be permitted to continue. Photographic reconnaissance dictated a multiple force assault on the bush around Gã Formoso. It would use the large navy landing craft LDG *Alfange* to land six combat groups of Paras at Ganduá Porto, just west of and downstream from Gã Formoso, and two combat groups of Paras brought in two waves aboard six *Alouette III* helicopters from Bissalanca to envelope the site. The force would be covered by the two *Alouette* gunships, and the ninth *Alouette* would remain on alert at Bissalanca for medical evacuation. The remainder of the FAP resources would also be fully engaged. The Fiat attack aircraft would lead the initial air assault at dawn to maximize surprise, and these would be followed by T-6G Texans in close air support of the deployed land forces.[19]

The operation opened on 4 February with the air attack at 0610 hours. At 0620 the six *Alouettes* arrived with the first wave of Paras protected by the gunship. At 0630 the second wave arrived. At 0640 the landing craft disgorged its six combat groups in Ganduá Porto under the air umbrella of a gunship and two T-6Gs. By 0900 the advancing ground forces had overrun Gã Formoso and captured the PAIGC antiaircraft weapons and ammunition, as the enemy fled. Those in flight were attacked by the Dornier armed observation aircraft and the gunship. By 1300 the Paras had occupied the entire enemy encampment without resistance. At 1800 the troops returned to the landing craft and were in Bissau by 2100 that evening.[20]

This was a perfectly executed operation in that the Paras with close air support put the enemy to flight, destroyed his infrastructure, and eliminated the threat of the antiaircraft site on the Geba riverbank. Other light arms and hundreds of rounds of heavy machinegun ammunition were taken. Enemy losses were unconfirmed, but it was thought to be about a dozen, while there were no Portuguese casualties. On the other hand, many aircraft had sustained hits.

While it was a successful military operation, the enemy abandoned his equipment and fled to fight another day. Missing from the equation was any people-to-people program. When the local population passively allowed the enemy to install a dangerous weapon nearly opposite the capital, alarm bells should have sounded. This deafness would continue for the remainder of 1967, with Portugal following its exclusively military solution throughout the balance of Schultz's tenure. Three weeks later the Paras conducted Operation PIRANHA in the district of Cubisseco at the top of the Tombali Peninsula, in which eleven enemy were killed and much matériel was captured. Cubisseco lies about fifty kilometres northwest of the southern border with the Republic and represents a substantial enemy penetration of Portuguese territory. Nine months later in November the Paras conducted Operation PHOENIX 1, again in the district of Cubisseco, killing thirteen enemy and capturing matériel. A month following in December, again in Cubisseco near the village of Bária, the Paras captured substantial amounts of matériel.

At the beginning of 1968, as the defensive strategy of Schultz was struggling, and the PAIGC had become firmly established in the south on the Cantanhez Peninsula after four years of war, Schultz announced a series of actions to push the PAIGC off the peninsula. Among these was Operation CICLONE II in February. This action on the Cantanhez occurred around the villages of Cafal

The Fiat G-91 Gina attack aircraft in Guiné. Note the photoreconnaissance camera ports in the nose. (*Source personal archive Tomás George Conceição Silva*)

Dornier armed observation aircraft. Note the rocket canisters under each wing. (*Source personal archive Tomás George Conceição Silva*)

Alouette III gunship, view from the gunner's position. (*Source personal archive Tomás George Conceição Silva*)

and Cafine and resulted in twenty-eight enemy dead, nineteen prisoners, and some captured matériel. Later in March in Operation TUFÁO (Typhoon) on the Island of Como on the southern end of the Cantenhaz Peninsula the Paras killed three of the enemy and captured matériel. Yet these operations were essentially strikes and left a vacuum when the Paras returned to Bissalanca. The PAIGC continued to reoccupy the now unprotected area, and the problem of population support was never solved.

BCP MISSION

During this early period, the BCP was employed essentially in independent operations under the direction of the FAP. Typically the Paras, because of their airborne mobility, were called either to aid army outposts that were in difficulty or to engage an enemy group that was detected moving about within the territory. In its two initial years, 1967 and 1968, the operational activity was both intense and productive: 215 confirmed enemy killed and 87 captured. At the same time the Paras suffered eight killed and sixty-one wounded.[21] The BCP was recognised in April 1968, when it was awarded the Cruz de Guerra, first class, and the guerdon streamer was attached to the unit colours in a moving ceremony.

This use of the Paras as an intervention force was based in the *quadrícula* or quadrille system of managing a high-threat environment. Under this method each military region (Angola, Guiné, and Mozambique) was divided into zones that generally encompassed a number of districts. Each of these was further subdivided into sectors that might or might not correspond to a district. The sectors were again divided into zones of operation (*zona de acção*) and assigned to an army battalion commander and his companies. The commander normally directed the activities within his *zona de acção*.[22] The companies were each assigned and positioned in a zone. From time to time it was possible for the battalion commander to retain one company as a reserve for unforeseen circumstances, but normally his area of responsibility was so large that such reserves could only be maintained at the higher levels of command. The presence of the battalion and its companies in near permanent assignment to a specific area held substantial advantages in counterinsurgency, as it enabled the troops to become familiar with the human and physical terrain and the habits of the enemy. This would also enable the troops to cement an all-important relationship with the local population.[23] When the enemy attacked, he took advantage of this dispersion to isolate and besiege thinly manned outposts, whether they were villages with a local militia or a company-sized force. In such cases help was generally needed and needed quickly. The isolation of these quadrille units dictated a relatively hard life for the troops. They took great risks together and thus formed a bond that lasted a lifetime.

In the case of Guiné, there were two zones that became so active that intervention forces were employed in them constantly. Both represented attractive enemy corridors to the interior of the territory, one from the northern border with Senegal and the other from the south and the Republic of Guinea. In the north the area was known colloquially as the "Corridor of Guidage" after the frontier post of the same name. In the south the corridor was likewise known after Guileje, the village in the centre of the enemy infiltration route.

By late 1967 the overall campaign was clearly failing to address the insidious advance of the PAIGC, and towns, such as Cacine, Catió, Bedanda, and Gadamael, became besieged and isolated. As Lieutenant Alexandre Carvalho Neto, the military assistant to Brigadier António de Spínola would write, "The situation was absolutely catastrophic, on the brink of collapse. Bissau had become practically surrounded."[24] The President of the Republic, Admiral Américo Tomás, who visited Bissau in February 1968, returned to Lisbon to report that "the war was held by a thread."[25] Spínola confirmed this observation with an inspection visit of his own and described the situation as "desperate."[26] While these condemnations may be a bit hyperbolic, it was clear that Schultz's exclusive military approach was ineffective in the face of the civil organisation and support by the PAIGC. Its strategy was unquestionably winning the population and thus gaining it the ability to manoeuvre at strength within Guiné. This void in Portuguese strategy needed to be filled, and Spínola had his answer in a civil outreach under an umbrella of security. He assumed command in May 1968 and saw his first task as one of drastically reducing PAIGC military capability and tilting the balance in favour of Portugal.[27]

Brigadier António Spínola in Guiné. (*Source Archívo Histórico Militar*)

Spínola, who habitually wore the traditional monocle of a cavalry officer, brought to Guiné a broad portfolio of experience. His résumé included leading a volunteer force in the Spanish Civil War in 1938 and acting as an observer on the German eastern front opposite Leningrad in November 1941. In 1955, he was made a member of the Administrative Council of the steel concern Siderurgia Nacional in addition to his normal military duties and thus became a beneficiary of Salazar's strategy for managing his military through such appointments.[28] Military pay was poor, and to advance in pay and promotion, ambitious officers were often either removed from the immediate military environment or had their position enhanced by assigning them to lucrative and prestigious special positions. Normally these were at high levels of government or industry in both the *metrópole* and the *ultramar*, and it was these postings, promotions, and pay that Salazar controlled. Spínola thus had Salazar's ear and confidence.

When Spínola arrived in Guiné, all was certainly not lost. Under the aggressive and determined air campaign from mid-1967 onward, the PAIGC had been put on the defensive and truly weakened. It was swiftly forced to dismantle its large internal bases that were attractive air targets and vulnerable to attack and replace them with semi-permanent smaller ones that allowed more flexibility, mobility, and agility. These low-profile bases were supported by twenty-six exterior bases surrounding Guiné – sixteen in Senegal and ten in the Republic.[29] This air offensive had nearly paralysed the PAIGC, as entire villages had fled to neighbouring states and abandoned their crops. Without these, PAIGC troops were forced to forage for edible plants, and many began to question the war effort. The PAIGC now had to explain to fleeing villagers why they should endure death and destruction to feed its starving troops.[30]

On another front, Cabral had been intensely negotiating for aid over the last five years within the communist bloc, and after he had secured agreement for the Chinese to train his insurgent force at the Nanking Military Academy, he turned to the Soviets, who then agreed to supply heavy weapons. By 1965 war matériel was abundant, and technical help was coming from Cuba.[31]

Spínola on arrival implemented his psychological campaign for recovery in which the people and the army would build a better Guiné with improved health, education, infrastructure, and commerce.[32] This program was known as *Um Guiné Melhor* (A Better Guiné) and directed substantial resources toward social operations on the premise that by attacking the fundamental needs of the people through positive deeds supported by an oral message, the promises of the PAIGC would be directly challenged.[33] This concept proved to be valid, and the PAIGC saw the Portuguese program as potentially even more dangerous than Spínola's devastatingly efficient helicopter assaults.[34] These assaults were key in establishing a security umbrella under which a "heart and minds" program could function successfully.

GANDEMBEL

Following Spínola's arrival in mid-1968, he began intensive operations to clear PAIGC-dominated areas so that he could begin his people-to-people program. He did this through the designation of targeted areas as operational commands. Such temporary area commands were aimed at reinforcing the local quadrille forces with elite forces, such as the Paras, to roll back PAIGC presence and free the population from enemy control. As the former infantry officer

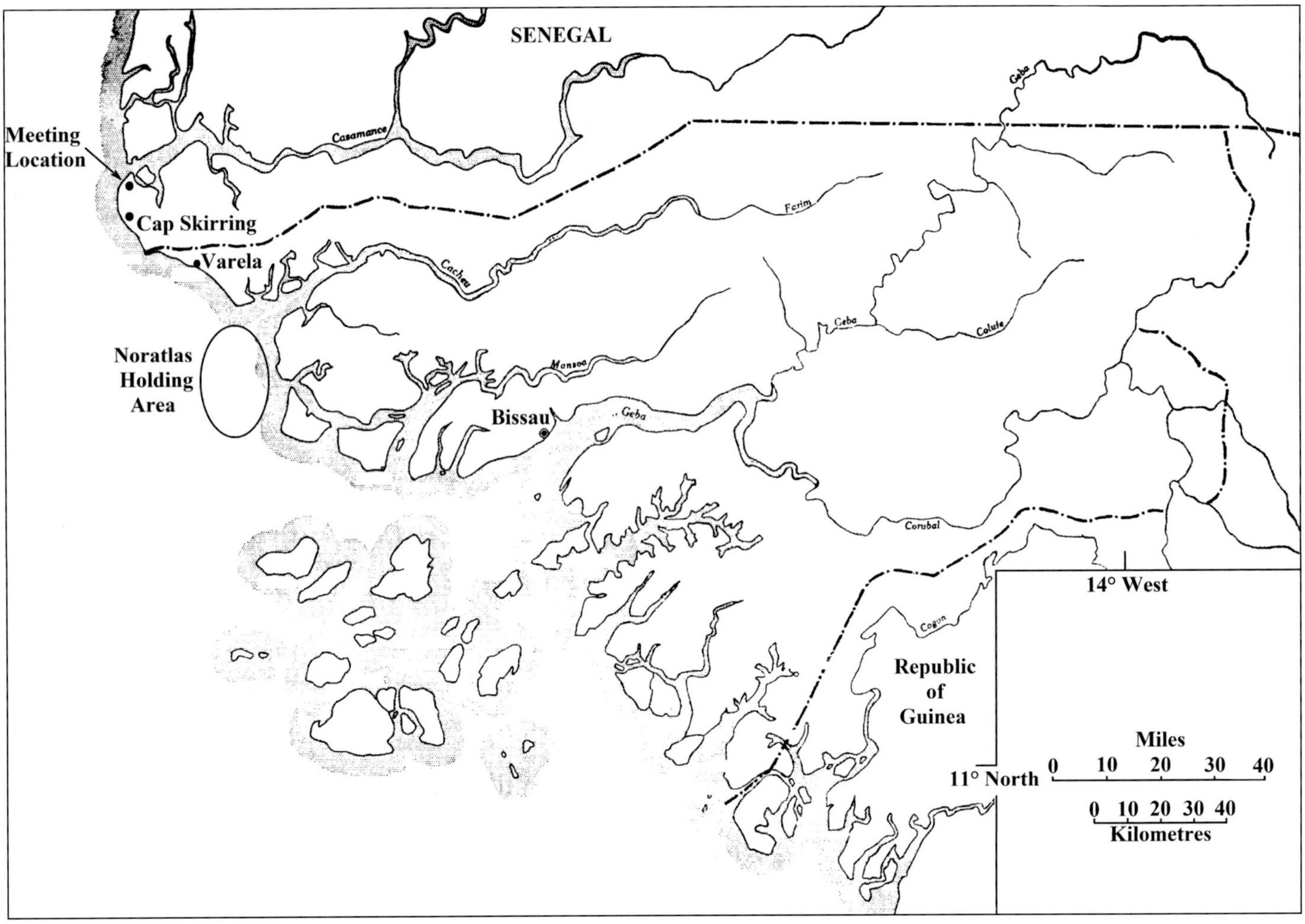

Covert operation to protect General Spínola while he was in Senegal. (*Map by the author*)

Alferes (2nd Lieutenant) Idálio Reis described the two groups of Paras who in early August 1968 arrived at his outpost of Gandembel, located three kilometres from the frontier and nine kilometres north of Guileje, they made all the difference in the morale and effectiveness of his troops: "The Paras were unquestionably elite troops better prepared for this type of guerrilla war and in an unrelenting pursuit of the enemy."[35] The Paras and the quadrille troops expanded the perimeter and fortifications of Gandembel in preparation for the action that was certainly to come.

On 19 August, Spínola created Operational Command 2 (COP 2) in the region of Guileje under the command of BCP 12 and the next day launched Operation JUPITER. The COP 2 area stretched along the southern frontier from Gandembel, Point Balanta, and Changue-laia in the north to Gadamael in the south. Spínola at first had doubts and considered withdrawing from Gandembel rather than initiating an offensive, as its proximity to the border and hence its vulnerability as well as the sparse local population made the effort seem a pointless use of resources, but then he changed his mind. At dawn on 20 August, the two combat groups of assigned Paras left Gandembel on a foot patrol in the rain and moved eastward toward the frontier, where they detected the presence of an enemy bi-group complacently bivouacked. The Paras surrounded the camp and surprised the enemy with a strong, well-planned assault that routed him and resulted in the capture of almost all of his armament. As the Paras returned along the trail to Gandembel, other enemy groups crossed the border, followed the Para tracks, and fiercely pursued them. The Paras mounted ambush after ambush against their pursuers, who returned fire as they were able, all the while suffering thirty-three dead and numerous wounded. When the Paras entered Gandembel, they were weighed down with captured arms and matériel.[36] Following this engagement, the enemy withdrew, and as it was quiet, the Paras moved to another assignment.

Toward mid-September the PAIGC began attacking Gandembel with 120mm and 82mm mortars from the far side of the frontier. The first barrage occurred on the seventh, and the second on the eleventh. In the latter case it lasted eighteen hours. The pressure of these bombardments and the behaviour of the enemy were a clear sign that he had capable observers who could see into the encampment. The PAIGC knew immediately the degree of success for each salvo, particularly by the number of helicopters that arrived to remove the wounded. The Paras quickly returned and on the fifteenth began a search between Gandembel and the frontier. Not far from the outpost the Paras discovered a wire that had been apparently transported to the observation site on two reels and reached all the way from a large, towering tree with a good view of Gandembel and its interior to a fire base in the Republic. This wire enabled the spotter in the tree to telephone the gunners and provide aiming corrections to the battery of mortars across the border. The Paras now conducted regular patrols along the frontier area from Gandembal north to Changue-laia, and life for the quadrille forces became routine. The PAIGC, however, broke this quiet on 8 November with 120mm mortar attacks, four bombardments in a single day. This was the last great attack on Gandembel, and the following two weeks passed quietly. The Paras departed shortly afterwards, the rainy season lifted the first week of December, and Spínola, who remained ambivalent about attempting to defend such a vulnerable outpost, ordered the base abandoned in January 1969.[37]

SPÍNOLA AND CABRAL

Beginning in late 1970, there were a number of developments that made the strategic resolution of Guiné possible and the likelihood that it could provide the key to an overall Portuguese solution to its wars. First, Spínola believed that Cabral was his own man and, despite a Marxist structure and philosophy in the PAIGC, wished to be free of Soviet influence in establishing a new regime in Guiné.[38] One solution to this desire was the offer of independence under some sort of Portuguese federation in which Guiné would be part of a Lusophone organisation similar to the British Commonwealth of Nations. With this concept in mind, Spínola began a series of overtures to Cabral through Léopold Senghor, the respected president of Senegal, in an attempt to end the war honourably for Portugal and to obtain independence for Guiné in a prudent way.

Spínola's strategy at this time was to reduce substantially the fighting capability of the PAIGC and to tilt the military balance in Portuguese favour. As time passed, Spínola's civil-military operations proved successful in checking the PAIGC progress and gaining the respect of its leadership to such an extent that negotiations for some form of self-government with a Portuguese alignment began to make sense. By 1972 conditions were ripe for negotiations, and at the end of April, discrete conversations were opened with a Senegalese minister to arrange a secret meeting with Senghor. This took place on 18 May at Cap Skirring a few kilometres north of the frontier in Senegal under tight security in which the Paras played a key role.

The need to protect Spínola while he met with Senghor and yet have his protection clandestine and unobserved by the Senegalese authorities presented a unique challenge. In concept the plan was to position an airborne force of some three hundred men over the horizon and out of sight and yet have that force able to engage in a matter of minutes with its close air support.[39] For this task CCP 122, CCP 123, and a portion of the headquarters company would comprise the ground force, and it would be supported by Fiats, helicopters, and Noratlases. A group of seventy Paras transported by twelve helicopters and supported by a gunship would be positioned at Varela just north of the mouth of the Cacheu River. The second group of eighty Paras would be airborne at low altitude in two loitering Noratlases just over the horizon. The Fiats would be circulating at high altitude awaiting a call. For operational security none of the Paras or aviators beyond the commanders of Bissalanca and BCP 12 knew the purpose of the mission.[40]

On the morning of 27 April two helicopters transported Spínola and a few select staff members to an airdrome north of Cap Skirring, and on landing all proceeded to a bungalow hotel next to the sea, where they met Ousman Camará, head of the Senegalese parliament. The meeting began at 0830 and was concluded by 1000 hours. Spínola detailed the reasons that he wished to meet with Senghor, and Camará affirmed that Senghor would act as a mediator between Portugal and the PAIGC with a view to obtaining a cease fire and peace. To further discussion Senghor would be happy to meet with Spínola in Dakar, but Spínola sought another meeting at Cap Skirring or in a neutral country.[41]

Some days afterward on 18 May, the operation was repeated, and Spínola met with Senghor at Cap Skirring. Senghor expressed great sympathy for Portugal and praised its social programs in Guiné, as he was well aware that many of his people south of the Casamance River were regularly crossing the border to receive medical attention from Portuguese doctors. Spínola explained his concept of Guinean independence, and Senghor indicated that he thought Cabral would be receptive and that he would act as an intermediary. This prompted Spínola to suggest that Senghor meet with Caetano in Bissau or perhaps metropolitan Portugal. Later on 26 May in Lisbon in a meeting with Joaquim Moreira da Silva Cunha, the Portuguese Foreign Minister, and Caetano, the proposal was rejected out of hand under the twisted rationale that such a move could not be controlled and that it would have grave consequences for the other colonies. He did not want Spínola sitting at the same table with Cabral, something that he saw as a humiliation. In Caetano's view, a military defeat was preferable. Spínola was shocked at such a warped position, and in his own words, "In reality, moreover, the last opportunity was lost to resolve the problem of Guiné with honour and dignity."[42] Contact with Cabral continued through his brother Luís Cabral into early 1973.[43] Spínola and many others remained convinced that Sékou Touré, the president of Guinée-Conakry, had an active hand in fomenting and supporting much of the internal dissention in the PAIGC in order to weaken the moderate Cabral in favour of a hard-line approach.[44] This activity led to Cabral□s assassination on 20 January 1973 and with it any hope of negotiating an honourable conclusion for Portugal and a prudent one for Guiné. Throughout these negotiations the pilots and Paras were entrusted with protecting Spínola and maintaining the secrecy of the meetings in Senegal. This they did well, as no one beyond those immediately involved knew. It remained Spínola's secret to reveal.[45] Meanwhile, the PAIGC continued to apply pressure militarily. Toward the end of 1972, Spínola decided that the enemy had begun to own the southern border areas of Guiné and that they needed to be retaken. The Paras would be returning to the south and to Cantanhez to sweep it clean of insurgents.

CANTANHEZ

The Cantanhez Peninsula had become an area completely dominated by the PAIGC, which had established a political and administrative infrastructure to govern the local population and a military one to protect its gains. The insurgent force was both strong and aggressive, and deployed in a way that enabled units to reinforce one another in the case of attack. The entire peninsula acted as an internal line in which reserves could be easily and quickly moved to counter any weakness. The PAIGC considered Cantanhez a "liberated area."[46]

In earlier attempts to drive the PAIGC from Cantanhez, Portuguese operations had been short and sharp and had only achieved limited gains. There had been no wholesale attempt to dominate the area with the social, political, and military infrastructure comparable to that of the PAIGC. As a consequence, the PAIGC claimed that this archipelago was "independent" and should be recognised as such by the UN, which had scheduled a visit to the area in April 1972.

Details of the April visit at the time were developed from intelligence that put it in the first week of that month but did not reveal the itinerary. Spínola consequently had to make a calculated guess and choose between two likely options: the region of Unal and the Corridor of Guileje, or the region of Cantanhez. He chose the first, as it was where the PAIGC First Army Corps was supposedly located, and assigned BCP 12 responsibility for the execution of Operation MURALHA QUIMÉRICA (Chimeric Wall) both to secure this assigned area and disrupt the UN visit. BCP 12 was reinforced by the First and Second Companies of African Commandos, two companies and a platoon of infantry, and a group from the Centre of Special Operations.[47] The operational plan focused on an assault against the PAIGC First Army Corps, securing the Corridor of Guileje, and patrolling the entire area of the anticipated visit. Portuguese forces would force the enemy into the open, where he would be annihilated or at a minimum have his security disrupted for the UN visitors.[48]

The operation began on 28 March and ended on 8 April 1972 and conformed to plan. The Corridor was secured with a dense network of ambushes; the supposed encampment of the First Corps was destroyed; and the entire area was densely patrolled throughout the operation. Various encampments that housed the PAIGC political and administrative infrastructure were destroyed. Intercepts of PAIGC communications talked about troop movements and resupply columns, but none of these activities were detected. There were many passing enemy contacts, but nothing significant. The enemy proved very defensive as opposed to his normal aggressiveness. When the operation terminated, there was a sense of frustration among the Paras, as they felt the enemy had deceived them, and their time had been wasted.[49]

Indeed, the UN observers had visited the length of Cantanhez during the operation, marching over trails and crossing small and large rivers in canoes, and were guarded by about four hundred insurgents. They met PAIGC luminaries, visited schools, and talked with the people in the region of Catió. In the UN report the observers declared Cantanhez "liberated."[50] Spínola had simply chosen the wrong area to target. Six months later Cantanhez became the new objective.

Spínola's plan for Cantanhez was to occupy the entire region, to expel the PAIGC, to regain control of the population, build roads, byways, villages, schools, health clinics, and anything that would improve the life of the population.[51] To effect this plan, in December he created Operational Command 4 (COP 4) to be led by BCP 12 and supported by a detachment of special marines, three platoons of artillery, an engineering detachment, a naval task force, and all available air support.[52] For the Paras, missions had always been about attacking an objective, conducting a patrol, or mounting an ambush to take prisoners, but this one was none of these. First, the force was to establish military cantonments in Cadique, Caboxanque, Cafal, and later Jemberém after building a road from Cadique to it through some very forbidding terrain. Second, the force was then to establish itself by persuading the people to accept the new order. Third, the force was to limit PAIGC military presence in Cantanhez and create a security umbrella under which Portuguese administration could function. Last, the force was to establish a psychological operation to support these changes, persuade the population to accept them, and draw the people into collaborating in the construction and improvement projects.[53] The flaw in this grand plan was the political position of the people. They were caught between the Portuguese and a ruthless PAIGC, which would come in the night and intimidate them. This struggle for the loyalty of the population was inevitably brutal, as the people routinely paid with their lives for any cooperation with the Portuguese.

The enemy stronghold was located at the headwaters of the Julole River, sometimes called the Calunelom River, a tributary to the Cumbujã River, on high ground, and from this headquarters he directed two bi-groups of about thirty men each, an artillery group, and ten groups of militia. There were also in reserve within a half-day march a sizable force scattered throughout Cantanhez. Earlier experience indicated the enemy could quickly assemble a large and experienced force and conduct a pitched battle to challenge any Portuguese intrusion. Further he had the capability to disrupt the logistics necessary to sustain a force the size of COP 4.[54] Nothing in this tactical picture boded well for COP 4. Regardless of the difficulties, Spínola was of a mind that Cantenhez was going to be reclaimed. For the Paras, Cantanhez was where they had historically

Airfield at Cufar, preparations for a large operation in early 1973. Cufar was the centre of war in Cantanhez. (*Source personal archive Abel Melo e Sousa*)

COP 4 headquarters and para encampment at Cufar in December 1972. The tents are protected by strong earthworks. (*Source personal archive Abel Melo e Sousa*

Construction of provisional huts in the reorganisation of the village of Cafine in February 1973. (*Source personal archive Abel Melo e Sousa*)

experienced their hardest fighting, suffered their heaviest casualties and greatest setbacks, and this would be so in Operation GRANDE EMPRESA (Big Company).

The operation occurred in two parts, the logistics and the operations. Both were complicated. The logistics line of communication began Bissau, and the bulk of supplies and troops came from there in large and medium landing craft operated by the navy. The nature of the terrain in Cantanhez and the inability of the large landing craft to navigate the small and sinuous rivers, such as the Buxanque, made it necessary on occasion to transfer cargo

Para encampment at Caboxanque during Operation GRANDE EMPRESA. (Source Museu das Tropas Pára-quedistas)

to medium landing craft that were able to negotiate the confined waterways. A depot was established at Cufar for this purpose.

Landings began on 12 December with Para combat groups being landed in Caboxanque, Cadique, and Cafal by helicopter. The Para reserve was loaded onto a Noratlas and taken to Cufar, where there was an airfield. The helicopters then began to shuttle Paras from Cufar to the three Para landing sites on Cantanhez. The naval fleet progressed up the Cumbijã River with the landing craft surrounded by their escorts. One army infantry company was put ashore at Caboxanque and the other at Cadique.

On landing at Caboxanque, the Paras immediately sought the targeted enemy encampment in the wake of an air bombardment. They were supported by a gunship, and the entire action was indicative of a routine precision exercise practiced so frequently that it was second nature to the helicopter pilots and the Paras. The resistance at the enemy camp was enormous, and a bitter struggle ensued. It was only on the third try after reinforcements arrived from Cufal that the Paras were able to take the objective.[55] Eight were wounded and evacuated.

The follow-on amphibious landing at Caboxanque went according to plan and without difficulty, as the enemy had been neutralised; however, at Cadique things did not go well. The designated landing site for the large craft carrying the road-building equipment turned out to be a *bolanha*, a swamp-like mud bank revealed at low tide. On disembarking from the LDG *Bombarda*, the vehicles proceeded about fifty metres before becoming mired in the soft mud. It took three days to recover the equipment and move them to their destination a kilometre away.[56]

Over the eight days following the Para insertion, they patrolled the region around the remains of the enemy encampment to prevent any counterattack. Despite the delay at the *bolanha* opposite Cadique, the operation had gone well because of a number of key factors: surprise, an effective plan, and adequate preparation. Plainly the enemy was surprised by the arrival of COP 4, and while he remained off balance, the force was able to establish itself. Matériel continued to flow to the landing sites, and the lesser priorities were entirely satisfied. As the month wore on, an additional infantry company landed at Cafal under benign conditions. This calm, however, did not last long. The enemy recovered from his initial shock, brought reinforcements to the area, and began to engage with hit-and-run attacks on the recently established encampments and generate frequent contact with the Para groups as they patrolled. To address these probing engagements the Paras formed combat groups and bi-groups to saturate a zone of operations, and this tactic created great insecurity in the enemy, as he felt that the Paras were blanketing an area where he had earlier enjoyed a free hand.[57] The Para groups actually moved in close coordination, using one group to drive the enemy into an ambush by another. This "cat and mouse" game required meticulous planning and tight control over each group, as they were operating in the blind in the elephant grass. It also depended on skilled map reading and elevated orientation skills, so that each group would be exactly where it was supposed to be, and the risk of fratricide avoided.[58]

Spínola gave instructions to all that the population was not to be molested. This was difficult initially, as each village had its PAIGC militia and was armed. The PAIGC had developed a strong link with

Vehicles disembarking from LDG Bombarda in December 1972 before becoming mired in the soft ground beyond. (*Source personal archive Abel Melo e Sousa*)

Burning the huts of an enemy encampment in an operation near Calaque in February 1973. (*Source personal archive Abel Melo e Sousa*)

Building the road between Cadique and Jemberém in February 1973. (*Source personal archive Abel Melo e Sousa*)

the population, and now the people were thrown into a quandary. Fearful, they fled their settlements and hid in the grass. When the Paras arrived at each of these, they found them abandoned. The danger here was that as long as the villagers hid, they remained under PAIGC control, for the insurgents mixed with the people. Thus when the Paras encountered groups of people, they encouraged them to return to their settlements where they would be safe. To remain in the bush with the hunted enemy was dangerous.

As the local people began to return, the Paras noted that it was the women, children, and elderly men. There were few young men, as those fit for military service had been pressed into duty by the PAIGC. Initially the people were fearful and hostile to the Portuguese, but when they were not molested and found conditions in their settlements improving, they relaxed and developed confidence in their new circumstances.[59]

The Paras now began the second phase of the operation, which was to reorganise the population. This meant building a series of protected villages with wells, cattle pens, health clinics, bath houses, and all of the other accoutrements of social support. All of this was delayed by the construction of the road. This was asphalted and stretched the breadth of the Cantanhez – thirteen kilometres from Cadique to Jemberém. It was completed under tight security and represented a strategic link between ports on the Cumbijã and Cacine Rivers. The new population centres of Cadique, Caboxanque, Cafal,

Launching helicopters in an operation in the Cachambas (an area in which all of the villages contained the name Cachamba) in February 1973. (*Source personal archive Abel Melo e Sousa*)

The paranurses took good care of the population. (*Source Museu das Tropas Pára-quedistas*

and Jemberém were now connected, and this link enabled new and enhanced commercial markets to develop. Spínola was pleased with the success of GRANDE EMPRESSA – so much so that he decided to extend the pacification to the north beyond the town of Bedanda to the villages of Chugué and Cobumba.[60] Occasionally the enemy would cross the Cacine and penetrate inland along the Chaquebante and Bomante Rivers to the region of the Cachamba villages south of the Cadique-Jemberém road and make passing attacks on the Paras. This was more of a nuisance than a real threat. Cantanhez became peaceful until May, when GRANDE EMPRESA was terminated and security was returned to the quadrille forces. COP 4 was dissolved, and BCP 12 was transferred to Gadamael and now faced an energised enemy fighting for another contested peninsula.

GADAMAEL

In the middle of May 1973, following the pacification of Cantanhez, the PAIGC was now more than ever using the Corridor of Guileje to advance westward in support of its interior operations and to move southward to maintain its subversion of the Quitafine Peninsula. Guileje represented a classic line of communication choke point and was in theory vulnerable to closure by the Portuguese. Its control was thus the Paras next assignment. On 8 January 1973 Spínola had designated the entire area between the Cacine River and the Republic of Guinea as COP 5 and established its headquarters at Guileje – a "hot" zone. COP 5 was commanded by Major Alexandre Coutinho e Lima, and was manned by:

1. A company of cavalry.
2. A combat group from an infantry company,
3. A reconnaissance platoon,
4. A platoon of local militia, and later
5. A platoon of artillery.[61]

The Paras, who were now in the "cool" zone of Bissalanca, began to prepare themselves psychologically for the fight. On 24 May, the besieging PAIGC force captured vehicles, cannon, and munitions in an enormous "rumble" at Guileje.[62] In fact the military installation at Guileje had been a lone outpost, and as soon as the PAIGC understood that it could destroy this outpost or force its abandonment, it brought artillery into range, supported its offensive with the overwhelming resources at Kandiafara, and began to lay siege. As the situation developed, COP 5 had garnered increasing enemy attention over the first four months of its existence. Beginning on 25 March, when the PAIGC downed its first aircraft with a Soviet *Strela* antiaircraft missile, air support became tenuous. It was also the beginning of the rainy season – something that limited resupply of the outpost, disrupted its communications, and hindered its military operations. As April passed into May, the enemy began to surround the base and reduce it with his artillery. On 18 May a force of two infantry combat groups and a platoon of militia was ambushed by a superior enemy force with an estimated strength of one hundred. Portuguese forces suffered one killed and eleven wounded. On 11 May, Spínola had visited Guileje and promised air support and MEDEVAC of wounded, a promise that would not be honoured. On 20 May, Coutinho e Lima flew to Biasau by helicopter to discuss the needed reinforcements requested by message earlier. Spínola told him that he would receive no reinforcements and that he must return to Guileje the next morning to be relieved by the Para Colonel Rafael Durão, the new commander of COP 5. Coutinho e Lima returned to Guileje on 21 May and found the outpost under violent siege, short of ammunition, and isolated from any help. In the period of his absence Guileje had been assaulted thirty-seven times. Because there was little question that the compound would be overwhelmed shortly, he organised a withdrawal of the two hundred military and five hundred civilians to Gadamael the next morning in the predawn. His selection of an unlikely route fooled the enemy, who continued to bombard the now empty Guileje and only entered the destroyed outpost on 25 May.[63] The Paras assignment to COP 5 was definitely going to be "hot."

When Coutinho e Lima arrived at Gadamael about noon, he was met by Rafael Durão and relieved. Rafael Durão by seniority became temporarily commander of the garrison at Gadamael and assumed responsibility for a force of about four hundred men now crammed into an area built to accommodate one hundred fifty.[64] In the nine days that he was commander of COP 5 and Gadamael, he expanded the perimeter and began regular patrols of the surrounding area. For an unexplained reason Spínola again changed his mind on the COP 5 commander, and on 31 May about noon, Captain Manuel Ferreira da Silva, a commando, arrived to relieve Rafael Durão, and by 1430 hours the PAIGC began to bombard the compound with 120mm and 82mm mortars, 130mm cannon, and recoilless rifles. This onslaught in which about eight hundred rounds of various types fell within the football-field size redoubt left the new commander in the gravest of situations and at a distinct disadvantage, as having just arrived, he had no understanding of the situation, did not know his commanders or their men, and had no plan of defence. There was no artillery, no air support, no doctor, and no exterior communications except for a small radio that held intermittent contact with Cacine.[65]

CCP 123 landing at Gadamael in June 1973. (*Source Museu das Tropas Pára-quedistas*)

Paras and quadrille troops expanding the defences at Gadamael in June 1973. (*Source Museu das Tropas Pára-quedistas*)

It is difficult to imagine a worse situation for a new commander.

On 1 June CCP 122 and CCP 123 were ordered to Gadamael, and at the same time yet another new commander was appointed for COP 5, Major Mascarenhas Pessoa. CCP 122 was landed at dawn on 3 June with the major, and he relieved Ferreira da Silva. The compound was soon under attack, as dawn gave way to daylight. The Paras took refuge in a trench system and watched, as the enemy maintained continuous fire and walked his bombardment the length of the fortification. Even when the fire subsided, it was clear that the enemy held the compound under observation. During these periods of relative quiet the Paras reorganised their defence. That afternoon a bi-group of Paras conducted their first patrol outside of the Gadamael perimeter, while the remainder maintained protection of the compound. As soon as the Paras left the fortification, they were taken under fire, and it was obvious that the enemy was close at hand. Departing and entering the compound was difficult over the next several days, hence the Paras developed a technique in which they would move outward until contact was made, then break it and call for artillery fire on the point of contact. Gradually over a period of hours the enemy was pushed away.[66] Nevertheless, the situation in Gadamael remained unsustainable, and it was on 5 June that CCP 123 and the commander of BCP 12 came ashore from a naval landing craft to bolster the defences. Still in light of enemy activity, more would be needed, and CCP 121 was positioned at Cacine as the reserve.

In the middle of the campaign and with the difficult history of Guileje and Gadamael, Spínola decided that perhaps Gadamael should be abandoned and proceeded to craft a directive to be hand-delivered by the naval logistics force supplying the base. When received, the Paras initially believed this to be a practical joke, but indeed it was confirmed and then modified by radio.[67] The Paras assured Spínola that all was under control and were allowed to stay. Fearful that Spínola would pay them a surprise visit, the Paras set about with the quadrille troops making the compound neat and expanding and improving its perimeter to accommodate the three companies – work all done by hoe and shovel. While one company was resting and refitting in Cacine, the other two were manning the ramparts at Gadamael, all in periodic rotation.

On 24 May a PIDE/DGS agent noted that his source in Conakry had revealed the arrival of a Chinese merchant ship with a load of arms. Among the noteworthy items were Chinese 130mm towed field guns, Type 59, with a range of more than twenty-seven kilometres. The PAIGC now had this artillery classic in addition to its rockets, recoilless rifles, mortars, antiaircraft artillery, and antiaircraft missiles. Further, there were at least ten PAIGC infantry bi-groups of between eighty and a hundred men each plus other unidentified specialised units moving to Gadamael.[68]

The initial Para tactical strategy was to gain control of the canal leading from the Cacine River to Gadamael. This was important, as it was the only line of communication to the exterior. The Paras began by neutralising the PAIGC positions overlooking Gadamael and thus robbing the enemy of his targeting intelligence. The going was hard, as the enemy bi-groups were probing the Gadamael defences and skirmishing with the Paras. The front lines were thus quite fluid, and this made artillery and air targeting very difficult.[69] Again the tactic of saturating an area first with fires, forcing the enemy to abandon it, and then occupying it with Paras on the lifting of the barrage proved successful. Repeated consistently, this forced the PAIGC to withdraw south-eastward towards the frontier and place his artillery within the Republic of Guinea. His engagement with the Paras was now with long-range artillery and short, sharp infantry clashes by small reconnaissance units. The artillery fire became inaccurate after 8 June, as a concealed and recently abandoned observation post was unearthed during the Para patrols. The back and forth with the enemy pushed him into his sanctuary, but the Paras were not done.[70]

On the maps and aerial reconnaissance photographs of COP 5, enemy presence was marked with red dots. The zone assigned

A PAIGC-manned Soviet ZPU-1 14.5mm antiaircraft gun of the type being used against the Fiats attacking the PAIGC bases in the Republic of Guinea. (*Source personal archive Tomás George Conceição Silva*)

to the Paras, however, was completely white and free of red dots. Peculiarly there was an uninhabited area with an isolated red dot just across the frontier and about ten kilometres southeast of Gadamael opposite Cacoca and Cacine. Aerial reconnaissance could not identify any base, but there were highly visible tire tracks around the suspected location. It fell on the Paras to reconnoitre the area, and on the moonless night of 23 June, CCP 121 crossed the canal next to Gadamael, waded through the grass in silence, and proceeded to the suspected site across the frontier. Here the Paras found the identified tracks of a large truck together with tracks from many other vehicles – all running parallel to the frontier or leading away from it. The Paras set an ambush to stop a truck and learn of its movements; however, after some time had passed without success, the Paras continued toward the suspect site and suddenly heard voices nearby. Clearly they were next to an enemy encampment. Coincidently, in the immediate area a strong storm was brewing, and when it arrived, it was hoped that it would provide cover for an attack. When the tempest began, the noise and deluge of rain allowed the Paras to surprise the larger enemy force, enter his encampment, produce many casualties, and capture a great deal of matériel. As daylight broke, the Paras saw a well organised and fortified compound and called for air strikes to destroy it and the others along the border.[71]

These attacks forced the enemy to react, and he did so with massive long-range artillery barrages of Gadamael on 30 June and again on 2 July. There was also at the time a constant stream of antiaircraft fire aimed at the attacking Fiats. The Paras could easily

The gateway to the casern of Parachute Battalion 32 in Nampula. (*Source personal archive of Fernando Pacheco*)

hear this din several kilometres away, then suddenly the sound changed to that of an apparent downpour of rain accompanied by some small explosions. However, it was not rain, it was the falling of spent explosive antiaircraft rounds. The Paras returned to Gadamael without incident.[72]

Also in the days following, the PAIGC began engaging the Paras in skirmishes on a consistent basis and suffered regular losses in these encounters as well as from the heavy air bombardment of its mobile fire bases. At this point the battle for Gadamael was definitely won. The Paras had suffered two dead and thirty-five wounded

Coat of Arms of Parachute Battalion 31. (*Source Museu das Tropas Pára-quedistas*)

Coat of Arms of Parachute Battalion 32. (*Source Museu das Tropas Pára-quedistas*)

out of a total of eighteen killed and seventy-six wounded over the campaign.[73] There was to be no reoccupation of Guileje, as it was too vulnerable. After training replacement troops, CCP 121 and CCP 122 returned to Bissau on 7 July, and CCP 123 followed ten days later.[74] The key to success at Gadamael had been the integration of the forces defending the outpost and its surrounds. The Paras and the quadrille forces combined to fortify Gadamael and extend its security perimeter with effective patrols. Further, the naval landing craft that were the logistics tail braved enemy ambushes along a twenty-five kilometre branch of the Cacine to maintain the outpost. Air support was there when needed. Success at Gadamael was a true team effort.

At the point of Spínola's disappointing meeting with Caetano in May 1972, he had gained enough credibility with Cabral to bring him to the negotiating table, a situation about as propitious as one could achieve in the besieged environment of Guiné. Any conflict resolution would now have to come from another direction, and the war laboured on for another twenty-three months until 24 April 1974, when middle-ranking Portuguese officers effected a coup and toppled the Caetano government. In 1975 Portugal granted Guiné its independence, and the PAIGC assumed control of the country.

CHAPTER 4
MOZAMBIQUE

Mozambique was the only theatre with two battalions of Paras, BCP 31 and 32. BCP 31 was authorised in November 1962 and deployed initially to Lourenço Marques and in November 1966 moved permanently to the airbase in Beira, after Britain threatened to put a strike force ashore there to prevent oil being delivered to its breakaway colony Rhodesia. Before moving to Beira, the Paras were often flown the 2,000-kilometre distance to the north to engage an active enemy. BCP 32 was authorised in November 1966 and stationed in Nacala at the airbase there. Both battalions were composed of a headquarters and support company and two Para companies, CCP 1 and CCP 2.[1] Once it became apparent that the British would not attempt to put troops ashore, the Paras in both Beira and Nacala exclusively engaged the enemy.

A DIFFICULT THEATRE

Mozambique, the third and final theatre, was situated on the east coast of Africa and fronted on the Indian Ocean. The territory stretched some 2,000 kilometres along the coast and the land rose as one moved inland from the sea. Its interior borders were shared with Tanzania in the north and with Malawi, Zambia (formerly Northern Rhodesia), Rhodesia (the future Zambabwe), South Africa, and Swaziland, as one moved south. The climate in the northern littoral was hot, humid, and inhospitable. In the Maconde Plateau, the Serra Mapé, and the District of Tete, the foothills and mountainous areas were very steep and random. There was often little foliage to offer protection from the sun, and in the dry season that runs between May and October, it was difficult for the Paras to find water.[2] In the south below the Save River the climate is milder, and here as the land rose toward the higher interior elevation, the weather became cool and dry. The lower elevations of the south were predominated by tall grass and savanna vegetation, and this gave way to abundant forest to the west. There were numerous rivers that converged into four principal ones that emptied into the Indian Ocean: the Rovuma, the Zambesi, the Save, and the Limpopo.

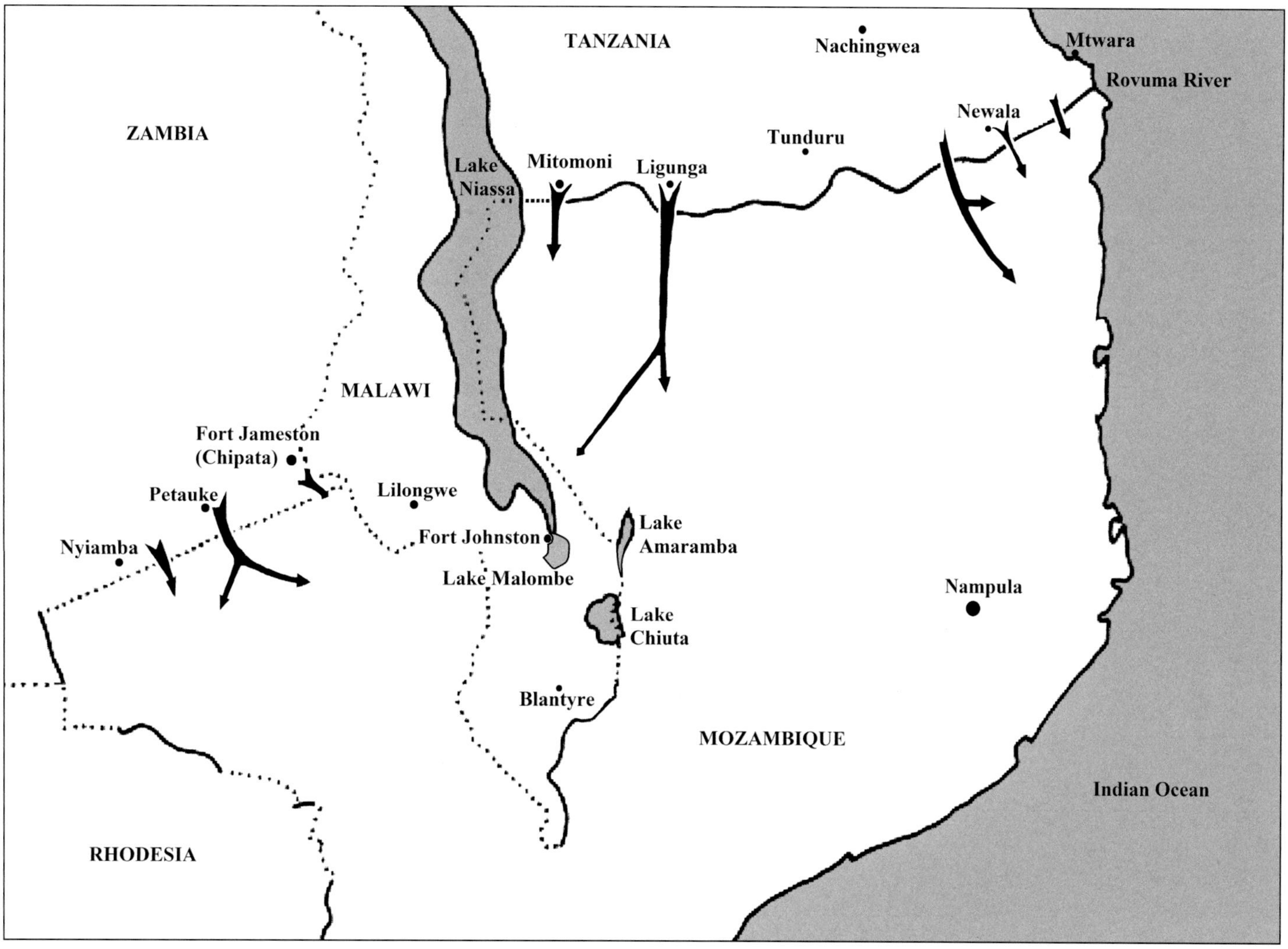

FRELIMO Lines of Penetration and Territorial Organisation. (*Source PIDE/DGS archives*)

The majority of the population was African and divided among a number of groups, of which the Maconde was the most important to the conflict, as these people straddled the border with Tanzania. Prior to Tanzanian independence, the border was open, and the Maconde in Mozambique communicated freely with their kin in Tanganyika. When Tanzania became independent in 1961, the border was closed, and formerly unhindered communication was now restricted. The Maconde, a warlike people who had successfully resisted British, German, and Portuguese efforts at pacification, were now ready to fight the Portuguese to re-establish intra-tribal communication.

FRELIMO

In Mozambique there were several exile, very small, nationalist organisations prior to 1961. The Portuguese government made every effort to dampen the spirit of nationalism in its formative stages; however, there were at any one time perhaps half a million Mozambicans, or about ten percent of the population, working in neighbouring countries. This group was exposed to new political ideas and in the period 1958–1960 began to organise themselves into associations with the goals of social contact, self-help, and ultimately national politics. These were united in September 1962 in the wake of the 1961 Casablanca Conference and at the urging of Julius Nyerere, the Tanganyikan leader, into FRELIMO (*Frente de Libertação de Moçambique*, or Front for the Liberation of Mozambique), making it the single strongest and most important movement.

Eduardo Mondlane assumed its leadership, and it is thought that he was selected by Nyerere when he was a UN researcher on trust territories before he joined the Syracuse University faculty. He, too, absorbed the lessons of 1961 and was not prepared to launch a guerrilla war until some three years later in September 1964, after his small force based largely on the Maconde was trained.

Stirrings had begun at Mueda in the Cabo Delgado district on 16 June 1960, when there was a hostile presentation of grievances to the district governor at the traditional *banja* or tribal meeting that degenerated into an intimidation of the authorities. The frightened security force fired on the crowd with resulting casualties, and reputedly seventeen Africans were killed in this demonstration.[3] This "massacre," which had been instigated by foreign "military counsellors" in Tanzania, politicised the Makonde people and pushed FRELIMO toward an armed struggle as the only solution to its border problem.[4]

FRELIMO initiated hostilities on the evening of 24 September 1964 with an assault on the residence and secretariat of the small administrative post or *posto* of Cobué in the Niassa district. The following day the naval launch *Castor* (P 580) was fired upon while on patrol in Lake Niassa, and the *posto* in Chai, on the southern edge of the Makonde Plateau in the Cabo Delgado district, was assaulted. Later in December, the *posto* in Olivença, just north and east of Cobué, was attacked.

Initially, the FRELIMO military strategy called for assaults on the Cabo Delgado and Niassa Districts in the north of Mozambique opposite Tanzania and a second front in the Tete District in the northwest opposite Malawi and Zambia, when both received their independence in 1964. However, a lack of support from these

Eduardo Mondlane attending 1st Party Congress, September 1964, Tanzania. (*Source FRELIMO)*

countries, a difficult logistics problem for revolutionary power projection, and a scarcity of people in Tete and Niassa to proselytise forced FRELIMO to restrict itself initially to Cabo Delgado and the Maconde Plateau. Its campaign there met with regular disappointment.[5]

FRELIMO had commenced operations with only a handful of trained combatants, and its first moves were tentative in that its leadership was divided over the nature of its campaign.[6] The internal divisions were in part generated by military failure on the single northern front five years into the conflict, and dissention grew so great that disaffected elements ultimately assassinated Mondlane on 3 February 1969. Portuguese observers pointed to the culprits as Maoist elements in FRELIMO and their growing opposition to Mondlane's pro-West position; however, these internal squabbles continued for years after Mondlane's death and resulted in stinging reversals militarily and a tendency to settle internal scores in blood.

FRELIMO had begun with a planned program of infiltration, subversion, and intimidation of the population, and raids against Portuguese infrastructure. There was the hope of mass insurrection against the Portuguese authorities, again in the vein of Holden Roberto's logic, but the population was too sparse, dispersed, and divided for this course to be a realistic expectation. The Makonde in Mozambique, for instance, did not necessarily share the revolutionary fervour of their kin across the border. Some Makonde were persuaded to join FRELIMO; however, true to their traditions, many rejected this intrusion and were subjected to the standard tools of terror, such as, murder, torture, and selective kidnapping, when they did not provide active help. In 1973 Neil Bruce made the observation that, according to defectors, more than 450 Makonde had been murdered by FRELIMO, 1,000 wounded, and 6,500 captured since 1964.[7] The accuracy of these figures is less important than the fact that atrocities were being committed on quite a large scale by African against African. In a country of nine million people, the population was composed of nineteen tribes and seventeen different language groups. For FRELIMO, it was important to create a broad popular base across these myriad factions, and yet its practices destroyed any genuine hope of doing so.

PORTUGUESE COMMANDERS

The first Commander-in-Chief of the Armed Forces in Mozambique, General João Caeiro Carrasco, failed to gain control over the developing situation in the north with his conventional approach and its lack of subtlety. His actions encouraged the local population to flee to areas less accessible to military and civilian authorities, as the people were frightened by his heavy-handed military actions and consequently gave their support to the traditional chiefs who were behind the emerging nationalist organisations.[8] Carrasco directed the war from his headquarters in Lourenço Marques, about as far as one could get from the fighting and remain in Mozambique, and concentrated most of the troops and services in the south. When his troops moved north and did engage, it was generally on a conventional scale against well-trained insurgents. Portuguese troops met judiciously placed enemy ambushes and the coordinated and sweeping fire of automatic weapons hidden in the bush. It should be noted that this modern form of subtle warfare was alien to the African character, which tends to be basic and direct. Africans have traditionally employed frontal attacks mustering hundreds of warriors with a disregard to the potential for casualties. The adaptation to this indirect method reflected the influence of seasoned foreign instructors.[9] The enemy proved numerous, motivated, well-armed, well supplied with munitions, and completely at ease in Cabo Delgado.

In August 1965, a new ground force commander, Brigadier Francisco da Costa Gomes, was appointed, and the following month General António Augusto dos Santos relieved Caeiro Carrasco as overall commander. These two new generals transferred their commands to the north to be next to the primary area of operations and created a Northern Intervention Zone (*Zona de Intervenção Norte* or ZIN) with headquarters in Nampula. The districts of Niassa and Cabo Delgado were designated as Sectors A and B respectively and each was commanded by a general officer. Within these sectors the army established a checkerboard or quadrille network of companies and battalions to blanket the terrain, particularly the area next to the Tanzanian frontier.[10]

This deployment of forces was the product of an operational concept that sought to interdict the FRELIMO insurgents as they initially crossed the Rovuma River and to bar their progress southward. A second barrier was established at the Messalo River, and a third at the Lúrio River.[11] The effect of these three barriers was to stalemate FRELIMO in the north and limit its advance to the border area and the Maconde Plateau. Within the sectors intervention forces would hunt the invaders.

INVASION THREAT

In November 1965, a few weeks after Prime Minister Ian Smith led Rhodesia to its Unilateral Declaration of Independence (UDI), the UN Security Council passed its resolution 217, which called on all member states to withhold recognition of Rhodesia, refuse assistance to its government, sever economic relations with it, and embargo petroleum shipments to the former colony. This resolution would serve as the basis, however flimsy, for the subsequent British maritime blockade and the expectation that other member states would cooperate. In December, Britain banned selected imports from Rhodesia and prohibited the export of British oil to it.[12]

This set the stage for the initiation of the British naval blockade as part of a maritime embargo. Already, however, there were holes in such a plan, as Rhodesia received oil via three routes: by road across Beit Bridge from South Africa; by rail through South Africa or Mozambique from either Durban, Port Elizabeth, or Lourenço Marques; and by pipeline from Beira to the Rhodesian refinery at Umtali. The British did not have the resources to block all of these routes, and thus there was grave concern over "seepage" and "serious leaking in the oil sanctions machinery" that would enable Rhodesia to circumvent the oil embargo with increasing effectiveness.[13]

By February 1966, there were indications that a Greek-registered tanker was headed for Beira with oil for Rhodesia, the *Joanna V*. Britain swung into action and committed an aircraft carrier, two frigates, and a support ship to close Beira to Rhodesian-bound oil. The blockade crisis began on 1 April, when a British aircraft initially sighted the *Joanna V* steaming northward toward Beira, and the Royal Navy warned it not to enter port. The Greek government refused permission for the British to board the merchant vessel, and the *Joanna V* continued toward Beira. The British warned that force would be used to prevent the discharge of oil at Beira, saying that the *Joanna V* "will be the first and last to enter Beira."[14] In defiance of the British, the *Joanna V* anchored two miles offshore in Beira roads. Britain, determined to prevent the discharging of oil, pressured Portugal. Portugal claimed neutrality and reiterated that it would not supply oil to Rhodesia, or acquire oil in the name of Rhodesia, or transport it in Portuguese ships.[15] Portugal went on to say that it was not prepared "to assume the role of culprit in a situation for which it formally and categorically rejects any responsibility."[16] Whereupon Britain obliquely threatened to use extreme measures to prevent the oil from being transferred ashore. Salazar was unwilling to run the risk of seeing English troops ashore in Beira and face another Goa. At the time that Goa was taken by India on 19 December 1961, the anti-colonial government of Great Britain had approved of the action, so Salazar took British colonial hostility seriously. This threat of force prompted the Portuguese to reinforce Beira with aircraft and crack troops.

On 14 April, the Portuguese moved BCP 31 into Beira and seized the *Joanna V*. These moves denied the British the option of a simple "police" strike ashore. Even so, Portugal realised it would be foolish to deepen the crisis, and in a series of meetings between Ian Smith and several Portuguese diplomats, it was agreed that Rhodesia did not need oil from the *Joanna V*. This resolved the flashpoint, and Britain appeared to have won the "Battle of Beira," but it was an empty victory. It had earned the enmity of the Portuguese, and they would now happily assist Rhodesia to evade sanctions without conscience.[17] Both South Africa and Portugal continued to facilitate the delivery of oil to Rhodesia by train from Port Elizabeth and Durban in South Africa and Lourenço Marques in Mozambique.

PARA EXPERIENCE

With the crisis past, the Paras now settled into their new caserns and began to operate in cycles from Beira and Nacala. During these cycles they were in various deployed roles in the difficult frontier area for between thirty and ninety days and then returned to their caserns to recover and act as intervention forces for the quadrille units.[18] Often with these deployments there was no defined objective, and the Paras were free to patrol areas favoured by the enemy to search for his hidden encampments, destroy his supplies, and to gather intelligence. If they could take a prisoner, this might yield valuable, immediately actionable intelligence.[19]

In other cases an operation might consist of an assault on a specific objective. This might be a fixed base or the ambush of a known enemy group passing through a specific locale.[20] Whether patrolling or executing a discrete task, the Paras moved in complete silence and used only hand signals or a whisper directly into the ear to communicate. Smoking was clearly forbidden, as it could alert the enemy. The glow of a lit cigarette was easily seen at night, and the smell of tobacco burning was distinct and obvious. In advancing through the bush, the Paras always experienced great anxiety, particularly those who were leading the combat group, as they had to part the often dense foliage constantly and carefully in order not to alert the enemy. It was crucial that the Paras detect the enemy before he detected them. The tension was especially great when the Paras were following trails where the enemy was known to set personnel mines and booby traps. Here as the lead Paras searched for signs of enemy presence, they also had to keep an eye on the ground to catch the signs of disturbed earth – a sure sign of a mine – as well as checking the foliage for a wire or cord that would trigger a booby trap.[21]

In many zones, remembers then Lieutenant José de Moura Calheiros, each metre advanced, each step made, especially when one's foot was placed firmly on the ground, was very much a vivid adventure and a victory over fear – fear that a mine would detonate under your foot or a booby trap would be triggered by your body.[22] Metre by metre, step by step, each movement, especially in the area of enemy bases, was endless and a tremendous test of courage and determination.[23] Such a tension-filled advance was exhausting and necessitated a constant rotation of Paras as point men. This was essential, as after a period the Para at point would lose his edge because of the physical and psychological toll that fear took, and security for the entire group would be compromised.

When the enemy was detected, the Paras would approach slowly and silently to gain visual contact. If recent tracks were found, they would be followed until the enemy was close at hand, whereupon the Paras would prepare for an assault. It might take all day, but the procedure was to walk, stop, and listen – a constant repetition of the sequence. Listening produced a near permanent feeling of watchfulness – scanning aurally and visually as long as was necessary to feel confident in advancing.[24]

The greatest fear was to hear the click of the trigger of a booby trap. In the Serra de Mapé, the type of booby trap used by FRELIMO had a three-second delay, giving the Paras two seconds to run and a third to hit the ground in the hope of avoiding injury. In the case of an instantaneous trigger, little could be done.[25]

Calheiros notes that for some unexplained reason through experience in the bush the Paras learned to detect danger. They could feel when it was nearby. There were many clues, such as the type and state of footprints in the trails, disturbed vegetation, the silence of animals, the absence of birds, and the frightened nature of the monkeys or their total disappearance. These and other signs alerted the Paras, who sensed a complete silence ahead of them.[26] The Paras developed excellent night vision and could see and operate well in the dark. The great difference between night and day was the MEDVAC capability, for if a Para were wounded, he could not be evacuated until daybreak.[27]

When engagement with the enemy finally occurred, despite the

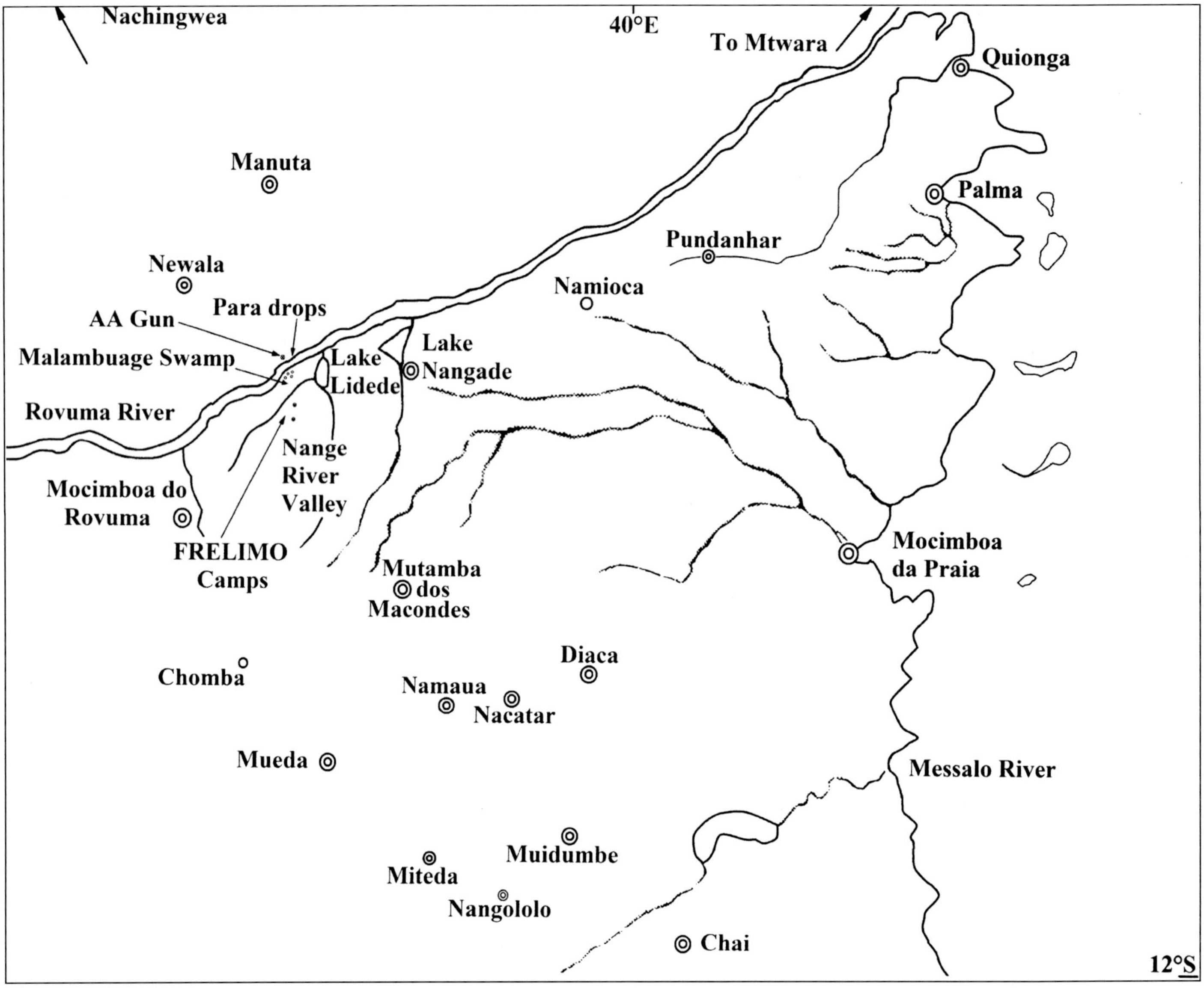

Operation ZETA. (*Source the author*)

The lead Noratlas as seen by José de Moura Calheiros from the LZ. (*Source Museu das Tropas Pára-quedistas*)

loud noises of shots, grenades, and mortars, and the smell of cordite, the Paras assumed an enormous calm, and their purpose was clear. All of their training and experience came into play, and they knew exactly where to go and what to do.[28] Immediately following an engagement, the Paras experienced an intense thirst and needed to drink a great deal of water. This could be a problem, if water was limited to the canteen a Para carried, as it often was in the dry season when it was difficult to find water.

The Paras operated in immense areas of dense bush and extensive savannas that were not fully understood, for there were no topographical maps worthy of the name. As aerial photography was scant, the Paras had to rely on a knowledge of the trails and landmarks, a compass, and the sun. In the end, their reconnaissance patrols were completed successfully with the tools at hand. There was also a radio which in the bush was the only link with the outside world – when it worked.[29]

When the end of the day came, the Paras sought a place to bivouac, preferably within the bush, and established a booby-trapped perimeter one hundred metres in radius. A dinner of field rations, supplemented by some manioc hopefully, was eaten, and the Paras then arranged themselves in an area free of scorpions, cobras, and bees and in an outward-looking circle to sleep. Five of the group stood guard at a time while the others slept. All of this occurred in total silence. Occasionally a large animal would take an interest, particularly if the Paras were encroaching on his territory. Sometimes a lion would circle them, and the Paras would then have their rifles ready for any attack. The sleep routine went well, unless someone tripped a booby trap, the enemy or more frequently an animal. If the sentries heard noise or detected movement, all were

Paras in the Malambuage Swamp. *Source Museu das Tropas Pára-quedistas*

Arms captured by CCP 2 of BCP 31 displayed in Mueda. (*Source Museu das Tropas Pára-quedistas*)

awakened. Rarely was anyone able to sleep afterwards.[30] These Paras conducted many operations, some mundane and others action-packed, that illustrated their capabilities. Operation ZETA remains one of the classics.

OPERATION ZETA

In April 1969, just four months after Mondlane's assassination, Lázaro Kavandame, a key FRELIMO figure, presented himself to the Portuguese authorities and revealed the location of the FRELIMO base Limpopo, which was the central logistics depot for all of the interior bases in Cabo Delgado with its Serra do Mapé and Vale de Miteda sub-depots. These served areas as far south as Muidumbe, Nangololo, and Chai, which is south of the Messalo River. Limpopo was an important enemy node and centre of gravity. The volume of arms traffic and fighters flowing through it was reflected in both captured documents and numbers of weapons seized in recent months, and by elements of the local population who described the enemy activity.

At the time it was the rainy season, and the enemy had become complacent, for the roads were largely impassable and movement of Portuguese troops was limited in the Maconde Plateau. Further Limpopo was surrounded by natural defences: marshy terrain with many escarpments and hills, scrub undergrowth, and water courses that became veritable cauldrons in heavy rain. Destruction and dismantling of FRELIMO lines of infiltration were key to crippling FRELIMO operations in Cabo Delgado, and Portugal aimed to seize on this new intelligence and the complacency of its enemy by having two companies of Paras assault Limpopo with an air envelopment and close air support during the period 6–11 June.

In planning the assault, the commanders faced a tactical problem in that there were not enough helicopters available to put the required two companies on the ground and in position to assault the base successfully. The solution then seemed to be a Para jump combined with helicopter mobility on the battlefield. The helicopters would act as shuttles in moving Paras from their LZ to the fight.[31] The planners likewise had to address two additional tactical difficulties. First, the only area near the objective suitable for an LZ was a small island in the Malambuage Swamp, located on the south bank of the Rovuma River between Mocimboa do Rovuma and Lake Nangade. Second, immediately across the river from the LZ on the north bank in Tanzania was an antiaircraft artillery battery that was well known and respected. This meant that only a single pass of the transport aircraft could be made safely over the LZ, but not a second, as the enemy gunners would be alerted. It was decided that the operation would proceed just after dawn, as the fog was lifting. Para Lieutenant Colonel Curado Leitão, commander of BCP 32 and the operational commander, gave the necessary orders. Calheiros would act as pathfinder and establish the aircraft beacon and light the smoke markers after being placed in the LZ by a helicopter along with some fellow Paras for protection. Calheiros had flown to Mueda to view the aerial photographs of the proposed LZ and noted that the island was small, and any miscue could result in the Paras landing in the swamp and possibly drowning or having to tangle with its animal residents. Further, the island was close by the enemy base, so the watchful enemy would be alerted.[32]

The ground order of battle was:

CCP 2 of BCP 31 (Beira),
CCP 2 of BCP 32 (Nacala),
Two platoons and a section of logistics from CCP 1 of BCP 32 (Nacala),
10th Company of Commandos, and
Two companies of cavalry, 2375 from Mueda and 2376 from Nangade.

The air order of battle was:
Six (approximately) Alouette III troop transports,
One Alouette III gunship armed with a 20mm canon,
Eight T-6G Harvards to attack the escaping insurgents,
Two PV-2 Harpoons for close air support,
Four Noratlas transports to insert the Paras, and
Three Dakota transports to insert the Paras.[33]

The 186 Paras in the two companies were prepared for a complex and dangerous mission, as they were the "hammer" in a "hammer and anvil" manoeuvre. The local quadrille forces, the commandos, and the cavalry companies would act as blocking forces.

The seven aircraft carrying CCP 2 of BCP 31 and CCP 2 of BCP 32 would arrive shortly after the beacon and flares were in place. The four Noratlases would be in the first wave and the three Dakotas in the second. After being landed with his squad of Paras, Calheiros activated the beacon to guide the transports, lit the flares to provide an indication of wind direction, saw the aircraft appear true to form, and thought to himself, "We are so good at this."[34]

Earlier in Nacala, the Paras had been suffering from the heat, as they sat in the mess at dinnertime slowly munching their plates of *carne de porco à alentejana* with a certain fastidiousness. Simultaneously in Beira the Paras had been working their way through their *bacalhau*

General Kaúlza de Arriaga being interviewed by a reporter. (*Source Museu das Tropas Pára-quedistas*)

com grão-de-bico in the certainty that it might be their last hot meal for some time. Although recently returned from the war zones, these Paras showed no reluctance to assume new missions when it became apparent that something big was in the works.[35] The week before, Nacala had become a beehive of activity, as Noratlases arrived with new equipment, boxes of field rations, cases of ammunition, and mountains of parachute gear. Secrecy was difficult to maintain for such a significant operation, yet surprise was critical for its success.

Now in the aircraft at the signal of the jumpmaster, the Paras stood, adjusted their equipment, and one by one quickly stepped into the slipstream passing the open door. The descent was rapid, and on landing, the Paras organised into combat groups to defend the LZ from an enemy they knew was now alerted. Some with bad luck landed in the mire filled with strange animals, but none complained of the alligators.[36]

When contact was made with the enemy, the fighting was initially fierce, and the Paras killed several dozen, captured about fifteen tons of war matériel, and surrounded the entire zone of the enemy encampments. During the three days that the Paras were on the ground, they consolidated dominant positions, combed the terrain between the Rovuma River, Limpopo, Balalé, and the southern reaches of the swamp. They raised mines, disarmed booby traps, and linked with army units that cooperated in a sweep of the plateau. The relatively new Alouette III helicopters were present in full and moved forces rapidly around the battlefield to outmanoeuvre the escaping FRELIMO cadres.[37]

In these days of intense work, a company of commandos located and assaulted an enemy logistics camp south of the swamp. The two cavalry units to the east combed the thickets next to Lake Lidede and the Nange River valley and assaulted an enemy hospital. Here they took diverse war matériel and documents, captured elements of the enemy and the supportive population. Another army company to the west of the swamp gathered the abandoned parachutes from the jump. Combing the swamp required an inordinate effort, and it was only through such an exertion that the Paras were able to achieve a memorable victory.

The elevated battlefield mobility of the Paras enabled them to inflict a thunderous destruction of the enemy infiltration and logistic lines of communication coming from Tanzania. The Paras found an impressive number of paths, trails, and hideouts spread across an area the size of about twenty football fields and linked across the Rovuma to a road that ran between Mahuta and Newala in Tanzania. The Paras destroyed his shelters, dismantled his encampments and logistic support, burned his huts and storage barns, and released his chickens and goats into the bush. However, there were some

Colonel Armindo Videira (left) and General Kaúlza de Arriaga (right) in a helicopter during Operation NÓ GORDIO (Gordian Knot). (*Source Museu das Tropas Pára-quedistas*)

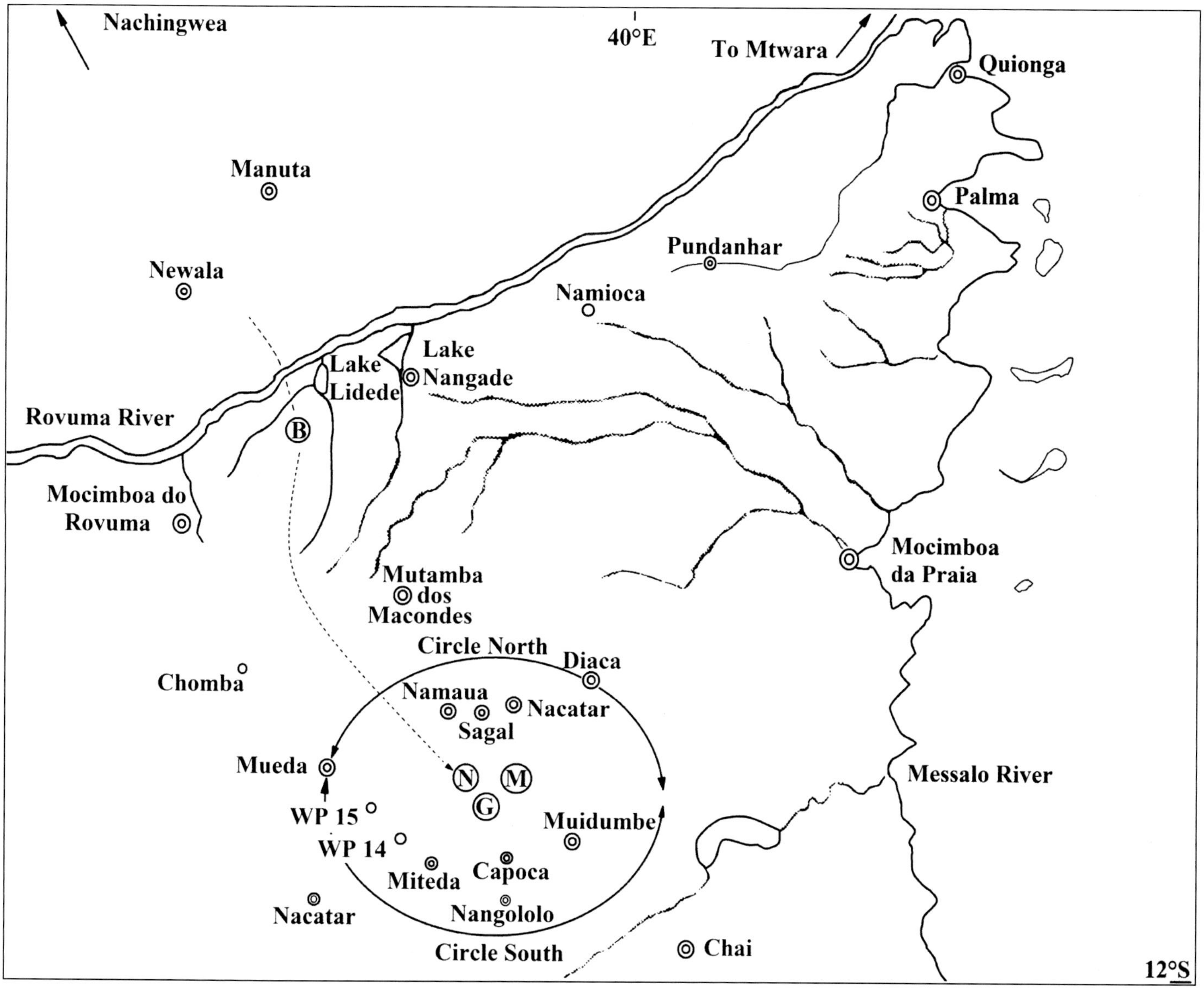

Operation NÓ GORDIO. (*Source the author*)

enterprising Paras who were able to evade the watchful eyes of their sergeants and hide a chicken in their camouflage uniform or their backpack and in the calm of the last day of the operation presented a dozen chickens to be grilled for their fellow Paras.[38]

The operation represented perhaps the most significant Para drop in Mozambique, as it was the first and largest operational drop in that theatre and one of a handful during the entire war. The aim of ZETA had been to overcome by surprise a series of enemy supply bases whose defences were completely oriented to a ground force assault and thus vulnerable from the air. In fact surprise was total, and FRELIMO forces generally fled in typical insurgent fashion. It was estimated that there were more than two hundred enemy routed. The bombardment inflicted by the attack aircraft on the fugitives softened their enthusiasm for combat and cut off their lines of flight. The insurgents acted predictably and after a brief fight disappeared in the face of a vastly superior force descending from the sky. They abandoned extraordinarily large dumps of weapons and munitions and made little attempt to hold ground. Normally their bases were in terrain that was inhospitable to a parachute assault and safe from Portuguese heli-borne forces with their shortage of air drop capability, so they were rarely disturbed.[39] ZETA was the exception.

AN OLD THEORY

In 1970 General Kaúlza de Arriaga assumed the duties of Commander-in-Chief of the Armed Forces of Mozambique and now faced a new hard-line FRELIMO leader in Samora Machel, who had assumed a more aggressive stance after Mondlane's death. Arriaga had for some time been anxious to return to the army from his duties with the Caetano cabinet, and he did so in the late 1960s. His initial operational command as a general was ground force commander in Mozambique, which he assumed in July 1969, replacing Costa Gomes. Here he chafed to command the entire theatre and pressed Caetano to remove Augusto dos Santos and install him. Caetano knew well that Arriaga had no experience in operational command, but as the last of the Salazarists, he was staunchly loyal to the regime. So in March 1970, Augusto dos Santos was reassigned as Chief of Staff of the Army, and Arriaga replaced him.

Arriaga's notions of how to fight the war differed from those of his predecessor in that rather than the constant pressure of ground patrols with aviation support within the quadrille, he envisioned a large conventional sweep of the Cabo Delgado area infected by FRELIMO. Augusto dos Santos and Costa Gomes believed that FRELIMO could be contained and victory achieved by the constant, indeed relentless, pressure of small actions that blocked the enemy

A portion of the "road" between Mueda and Nancatári to the southwest, heavily eroded by the rainy season. (*Source personal archive of António Silvestre*)

Unearthed booby trap improvised with three grenades and added rocks for shrapnel effect found near Mueda. (*Source personal archive of Armando Cardoso Martins*)

and gradually ground him down at a sustainable cost. From the time that Arriaga was a professor of military tactics during the academic year 1964–1965 at the Institute for Advanced Military Studies (*Instituto de Altos Estudos Militares* or IAEM), the premier graduate school for military officers in Lisbon, he advocated the attack in force supported by artillery and aviation fires as the preferred method of winning war, any war. This was a counterinsurgency theory that had been abandoned by most Portuguese generals and certainly was not held by either Rhodesia or South Africa, two allies in the insurgency wars of austral Africa.[40] Now with his first operational command, he had the opportunity to put this theory into practice and prove its validity.[41] He believed that such a grand operation in which the enemy was swept from the contested area was the path to victory over an insurgency despite the cost.[42]

OPERATION NÓ GORDIO

In June 1970, the small village of Mueda became the centre of the grand operation that Arriaga mounted to conquer FRELIMO, Operation NÓ GORDIO (Gordian Knot).[43] One of Arriaga's early moves in assuming command had been to establish the Operational Command of the Intervention Forces (*Comando Operacional das Forçes de Intervenção* or COFI) next to his headquarters in Nampula. Under COFI he centralised control of the Paras, the marines, and the commandos within Mozambique and in April moved it to Mueda under the command of Para Colonel Armindo Videira.

Arriaga's plan was relatively simple, but many adjustments had to be made in its execution because of the difficult terrain. For instance, the altitude of Mueda itself was 2,789 feet, and this required lengthening the runway by 1,200 feet to accommodate fully fuelled and armed attack aircrafts on their take-off roll. A further factor was the nature of the terrain. The principal rivers in the operating area were the Mueta, Litembo, and Muatide, all of which held water throughout the year and became veritable cauldrons during the rainy season. The roads in the area were deeply affected as well and were

Paras burning the huts at an enemy encampment. (*Source personal archive of Serrano Rosa*)

Paras on the road to Tete in December 1970. The rainy season can reduce a road to impassable mud in a matter of hours. (*Source personal archive of António José Guerra*):

Paras exiting a helicopter somewhere in Tete in 1971. (*Source personal archive of Tavares*)

hardly worthy of the name in the rainy season. Both the swollen rivers and the washed out roads would provide formidable barriers to manoeuvring ground troops and would require a significant number of helicopters. The valley of the Muera River, situated to the east of Mueda, constituted a critical area for Portuguese forces. Here the terrain consisted of mountainous areas with steep valleys whose slopes held tall impressive trees surrounded by grass. Along the riverbanks of these forested valleys the enemy had established its key bases and its strongest presence in all of Mozambique. From these bases attacks were launched on the surrounding Portuguese forces during the "Maconde Hour" – the hours of twilight when it was thought Portuguese forces would be vulnerable.[44]

The remainder of the terrain, particularly north of Mueda, consisted of shrub-like plants three to four meters in height that formed a dense, nearly impenetrable matted growth. It was a formidable barrier to ground forces attempting to manoeuvre, as this aggressive vegetation contained nasty briars, prompting the troops to nickname it the "zone of whips" (*Zona dos Paus*).[45] This difficult, enemy-infested topography was ringed with army encampments: Sagal and Diaca in the north, Muidumbe in the east, Nangololo in the south, and Mueda to the west. However, successfully flushing FRELIMO from its sanctuary was considered an unlikely occurrence with the normal contingent of assigned forces. Arriaga intended to fix this problem.

The concept of NÓ GORDIO called for defining the battlefield as the area encompassed by the villages of Mueda, Miteda, Nangololo, Muidumbe, Sagal, and Namaua. This was known as "Nucleus Central" and was surrounded by a circle of forces divided

In a moment of lightness General Kaúlza de Arriaga poses with Paras from BCP 32 in Nampula. (*Source personal archive of António José Guerra*)

in the North and South Circles. It was to be penetrated from the south and west from Water Posts 14 and 15 and the settlement of Capoca, as depicted on the battlefield map. The ground forces making the penetrations would be supported by aviation resources and combat engineers. Phased advances on the Bases Gungunhana, Moçambique, and finally Nampula (designated G, M, and N respectively) were expected to drive the insurgents to flee. To counter this, ambush sites were established around the perimeter circle on the ground and aircraft patrols initiated to kill or capture those in flight.

It was estimated that there were 2,500 insurgents in the targeted area and about 20,000 local inhabitants who were largely controlled by FRELIMO.[46] The insurgents had infiltrated through the logistics Base Beira (designated B) and established themselves in Nucleus Central. To sweep them from this wilderness, Arriaga assembled a force of 8,000 men and another 2,000 for the logistic support necessary to sustain them for the month-long assault, for it was on the scale of a conventional battle in the vein of World War II.[47] Indeed, the necessary resources came from every corner of Mozambique, and ultimately over the months-long operation an estimated 30,000 participated in one form or another.[48]

Beginning on 25 June, the FAP launched successive attacks on FRELIMO Base Lúrio, located south of Nucleus Central, as a diversion from the true targets of G, M, and N.[49] Throughout NÓ GORDIO, air operations were hindered by weather conditions and especially the morning fog. As the operation opened, the commandos attacking G were launched from Capoca and Water Post 14 and unable to locate it initially. After a day it was found abandoned.[50] The column of Paras from Capoca attacking M encountered stiff resistance and hard going with mines and booby traps. On reaching the camp, the Paras found it abandoned.[51] The marines attacked N and reduced an enemy force of sixty insurgents.[52] The COFI forces then proceeded to reduce the enemy base infrastructure and unearth arms caches. The large number of insurgents thought to be in Nucleus Central seemed to have vanished. Indeed at the first scent of NÓ GORDIO, they had used the local population as cover and melted into the flow of people fleeing the area and the coming fight.

(One of the most important helicopter operations during NÓ GORDIO was casualty evacuation. Integral to these operations were the para-nurses who assumed the same risk as the pilots in entering a combat zone and proved a providential addition in the care of the sick and wounded. They performed selflessly and showed enormous courage in discharging their mission. Many of these evacuations were "zero hours" (*zero horas*), that is, situations in which time was of the essence and the patient required immediate medical attention to survive. Sometimes these occurred end-on-end, and the nurses' spirit of sacrifice in the face of the fatigue associated with such operations moved all who saw them. In these cases particularly, the skills of the para-nurses as much as those of the pilots made a life or death difference.

Following NÓ GORDIO, FRELIMO largely reduced operations in Cabo Delgado and Niassa and shifted its focus to the west and Tete, where there was a thin and unfriendly population. The opportunity to penetrate Mozambique and reach the south through Tete, however, held more promise. While FRELIMO had been surprised by the scale of NÓ GORDIO, the largest operation undertaken during the war in any theatre, it was hardly defeated.

Arriaga was delighted with the success of his operation and spent Christmas of 1970 with his wife in a former FRELIMO base in the north. Caetano, however, was less delighted at the rising financial and military cost, and further such offensives were forbidden.[53]

Militarily, NÓ GORDIO was well executed but was a misuse of limited resources. These most certainly could have been used to better effect by devoting them to the classic counterinsurgency elements of policing the population and gathering intelligence on the enemy. The toll that it took on the troops and equipment was unaffordable in the long run from the strategic perspective.

The north of Mozambique was in itself a formidable barrier for FRELIMO, as its forces had to travel long distances over relatively barren land to find targets of opportunity. So even if the Rovuma River border was porous, and insurgents could wander almost at will through Niassa and Cabo Delgado, it was not a target-rich environment. The Portuguese held periodic offensives, the largest of which was NÓ GORDIO, to discourage FRELIMO, but the heart of Mozambique was south of the Zambezi River, some 1,000 kilometres away. To even the most enthusiastic FRELIMO fighter, the prospect of crossing such a vast expanse of hostile territory and relying on support from an indifferent population was daunting, if not impossible. With no victory in sight, a new strategy was needed to reach the Portuguese centre of gravity in the south.

In 1968, Zambia had given permission for FRELIMO to establish bases there. Following NÓ GORDIO, FRELIMO began to move its troops to Zambia and develop a series of bases along the Zambian border north of the Zambezi River and the Tete district of Mozambique. These forces transited Malawi, with its government turning a blind eye much to Portuguese distress.[54] Indeed, Al Venter notes that FRELIMO insurgents were traveling openly by the busload from Tanzania and were guarded by the Malawi police, who were making certain that they did not linger on the Malawi side of the border.[55] This development forced Arriaga to shift his attention to the northeast.

Tete was, like Niassa and Cabo Delgado, a sparsely populated area. Within the district, however, Portugal in 1969 had embarked on an ambitious project at Cabora Bassa (variously Cahora Bassa) to dam the upper reaches of the Zambezi River as a source of electrical power. The dam was also designed to open in 1974 and create an enormous reservoir 280 kilometres in length and 38 kilometres at its widest point. This source would irrigate here-to-fore dry but fertile lands in an effort to bring prosperity to Tete and ultimately Mozambique as well as block FRELIMO advances south into Tete. As it was, by 1971 FRELIMO was active in the area south of the Zambezi in Tête.[56] FRELIMO bases there also hosted Zimbabwean insurgents, a source of great concern to Southern Rhodesia, which began conducting "hot pursuit" operations into Tete. Arriaga consequently moved troops to Tete in an attempt to foreclose FRELIMO incursions in this district; however, Portuguese forces now were greatly overextended and faced significant difficulties in stopping infiltration completely. Neighbouring Rhodesia would now be drawn into Tete to help cover the Portuguese shortfall, as FRELIMO began to share its bases with the Rhodesian insurgency movements. In contrast, Niassa and Cabo Delgado became for the moment temporarily quiet.

UNFINISHED CAMPAIGN

With this overextension, it was easy for the insurgents to appear at inopportune times in very small numbers, and although the threat was modest and containable, it spread alarm because of the adverse publicity in the media. The main problem for both FRELIMO and Portugal was time – time for FRELIMO to undermine the government in Lisbon and time for the military campaign to provide the space for a political solution. Long ago FRELIMO had laid plans for this eventuality by infiltrating communist sympathisers

Eastern Military Zone and MPLA Incursion Routes into Eastern Angola. (*Source Arquivo da Defesa Nacional*)

into the Portuguese military and spreading pacifist ideas among the recruiting pool of university students who would later be the officers and unit commanders. As Portugal continued to make progress in its political solution in Africa, a cadre of middle-grade officers in Lisbon initiated a revolution in April 1974, and within a year the Portuguese military had abandoned Africa and the loyal Portuguese population to its fate. The urgency to find an expedient and quick political solution discarded common sense and the good that the military had accomplished socially and economically. Mozambicans thus became the greatest losers in both "independence" and the war that continued long after Portugal departed.

CHAPTER 5
VICTORY IN SIGHT

The Eastern Military Zone (ZML) of Angola was a vast plateau with an altitude of about 3,000 feet and an area of some 700,000 square kilometres (270,272 square miles). It comprised the districts of Lunda, Moxico, Bié, Cuando Cubango, and portions of Malange and was about seven and a half times the size of continental Portugal.[1] It was a wasteland for insurgent proselytising, as it contained only 1.3 million inhabitants or about five people per square mile. This latter figure was misleading, as the bulk of the population lived along the Benguela Railway (CFB) or in the primary towns, so in the bush there was actually less than a person per square mile. The goal of the insurgents, of course, was to penetrate far enough westward to where there was a denser population that would respond hopefully to the insurgent message and significant commercial infrastructure to attack. The problem with this approach was that it was a long and forbidding route from Zambia to the developed area toward the Atlantic Ocean, and much could go wrong.

Overall the ZML was a sprawling savanna sparsely dotted with trees. From the point of view of the insurgent, there were ideal concealment areas scattered through the more elevated land characterised by ravines and dense forest.[2] Both the vast savannas and semi-mountainous terrain posed significant policing problems for Portugal, for it meant that finding an insurgent column or small "squadron" in either setting was extremely complicated, and gathering the vital intelligence about its activities and intentions was an extraordinary challenge. When insurgent infiltration began in 1966, the army had four battalions there.[3] Even as troop numbers increased, the ZML was a big place that swallowed troops in great numbers in any attempt to maintain contact with the enemy. The key was the mobility and flexibility provided by the Paras and their helicopters.

INSURGENT STRATEGY

The MPLA from its new Zambian bases planned a two-pronged assault. The southern one would be mounted from Mongu, Shangombo, and Sikongo and known as the Route of the Cuando. It would follow this river valley westward with the plan of reaching the populated and wealthy district of Bié and the central plain of Huambo, the heart of Angola. From this point the insurgents hoped to control the entire country and to reach all the way to Malange through an axis of advance along the Cuanza River valley.[4]

The northern one was called the Route of the Luena, or the "Agostinho Neto Route" by the MPLA, and was to be launched from Chipango and Cassamba and aimed along this river directly at Luso and from there to the highland plain of Malange. The hope was to gain control of the Luanda-Malange railway, reach Luanda, and link with forces coming from the north.[5] These routes pushing out of the Salient and following the Luena River never successfully penetrated a front defined by an interior line connecting the population centres of Cazoa, Cazage, Cassai-Gare, and Lucusse with Luso as its hub.[6] The MPLA could muster about 4,000 men, of whom about 3,000 were armed. Its operations were centred around anti-vehicle and anti-personnel mines, forced recruiting and intimidation of the population, reaction to Portuguese assaults, and some bursts of fire at Portuguese military installations in hit-and-run tactics.[7]

Campaign plans for the UPA/FNLA are much less distinct. As in 1961, it attempted to reach economic centres where it could inflict damage. It was humiliated in engagements with both the Portuguese and the MPLA, and as a result lost key international support from the OAU.[8] By 1971, the UPA/FNLA had approximately 600 men on the eastern front of whom only about 400 were armed. Its offensive was abandoned in September 1972, because its forces were stalemated at the edge of Portuguese territory, checked by both the MPLA and the Portuguese in the north and east of the ZML, and thus stood little chance of success. Both UPA/FNLA groups remained relatively inactive as a means of survival.[9]

UNITA simply intended to establish a base deep in the interior of Angola and, using some notion of the oil-spot theory of expanding control, mobilise an ever increasing number of the population to gain the "total independence of Angola." Indeed, Savimbi was forced by circumstances into this improbable posture, claiming that a true nationalist movement should operate from bases within Angola, as in July 1967 he was finally and completely expelled from Zambia. Certainly the implementation of such a policy ensured his isolation. By 1971 UNITA was surrounded, and Savimbi counted fewer than 1,300 followers. In order to survive in defeat, he and his men came to an accommodation with the Portuguese. Between 1971 and 1973, UNITA activities were restricted to a prescribed zone at the headwaters of the Lungué-Bungo, and it agreed to cease operations against the Portuguese.[10] As part of this understanding, UNITA would receive arms and medical support and would be free to engage the MPLA.[11] By this time Savimbi had about 500 armed men.[12]

There were substantial weaknesses in the campaign design of all three in that their lines of communication would be long and vulnerable, or in the case of UNITA, non-existent. The goals of each would rely increasingly on the weak strategy of hope, as each moved further and further from its external support and progressively isolated itself deep in the hostile interior of Angola.

PORTUGUESE CAMPAIGN STRATEGY

In countering this multi-axis assault, the Portuguese were quick to see that UNITA and the UPA/FNLA would be easily contained and that the MPLA represented the real threat. They thus developed a three-phase theatre strategy. First, Portuguese security forces would check the expansion of the insurgent penetration. This would mean defining the population battlefield and bringing security to those threatened. Next, the security forces would surround the insurgents and limit them to a geographic area bounded by the Cuito, Cuanza, Munhango, and Cassai Rivers, in a front that ran from Dirico in the south to Teixeira de Sousa in the northeast. This was admittedly a substantial tract, but it was thinly populated by any standard and would provide little sustenance. The insurgents could thus do little damage in this isolation and would indeed slowly starve. Within it Portuguese security forces would relentlessly pursue the enemy, who would become increasingly harried and besieged. Finally in 1973 and 1974, as the cordon drew progressively tight, the enemy would be completely destroyed.[13]

The need for this lengthy approach was prompted by a number of factors. First, Portugal had limited manpower to police the vast region of the east. This limitation dictated an approach that enlisted the sparse terrain, geographic remoteness, and harsh climate as allies in isolating the insurgents in an attritional war. Second, these three regional characteristics appeared to favour the insurgent in that he could easily hide or move largely unhindered by Portuguese forces, so time was needed to track and destroy him.

From 1967 onward the BCP rotated one of its companies to the ZML to counter the infiltration of UNITA and the MPLA. These deployments were either to Ninda or Léua, both located near one of the established enemy penetration routes – Ninda on the Route of the Cuando, and Léua on the Route of the Luena. One of the first and most noteworthy Para operations in the east was mounted from Ninda into the area just south of Muié on the Dengue River, where the MPLA had established a camp.

A Puma helicopter collecting troops following an operation in a *chana*, an extensive plain of hundreds of square kilometres completely covered in tall grass in the east of Angola. (*Source Força Aérea Portuguesa*)

OPERATION EXARCO

Operation EXARCO (Exarch) was launched by the Paras on 25 September 1968 to reduce the MPLA encampment "Dengue," which was commanded by Manuel António da Costa Kiako with the nom-de-guerre of *Mundo Real* (Royal World).[14] The camp was located about ninety-five miles from the eastern border with Zambia and about forty miles north of the Cuando River. Intelligence from captured MPLA operatives indicated that there were likely key leaders conducting a planning session there following a regional assembly of eastern zone functionaries. The operation from the point of view of the MPLA was captured in an account by Ivan do Castro, whose nom-de-guerre was *Janginda*: On the morning of 25 September the day began for the "freedom fighters" at "Dengue" with a fog on the horizon, the traditional clapping, personal hygiene and the formation of all on the parade for the daily work assignments.[15] Everyone was told to be prepared for an attack, as it was thought that the base could not remain undetected for more than a week. It was not known if "Dengue" would be spared assault or if the Portuguese put much faith in the "confessions" of those they captured. Whatever happened, all were to be prepared and watchful. Among those present was Dr. Américo Boavida, nom-de-guerre *N'Gola Kimbanda* or "chief healer," a physician and director of medicine in the eastern sector.[16]

At 0700 the planning session began with four commanders present:

- Ivan de Castro (*Janginda*),
- Justino Frederico Katwiya (*Mwihula*),
- Inácio João Batista (*Massunga Kota*), political commassar,
- Bernardo Kapangue (*Likambuila*), logistican for the eastern sector, and
- Donald Barnette, a journalist.

Almost immediately everyone present noticed the distant noise of an aircraft engine and thought it was a Noratlas – popularly known as the "peanut" because of the shape of its fuselage. A few minutes later there were cries of alarm, as it was not a "peanut," it was an attack. The base commander gave the order for everyone to disperse.[17]

At that instant a Dornier appeared over the camp and launched three smoke rockets to mark the target. The next moment a PV2 Harpoon and six T-6 Harvards appeared and dropped their load of 250-kilogram bombs within the targeted area. Next a gunship raked the area with its 20mm cannon and paved the way for the troops arriving in the transport helicopters.[18]

When the first bombs fell, there was general bedlam with women yelling, children crying, orders and counter-orders. The first bombs fell in the kitchen and on the medical hut. Quickly "Dengue" emptied. Meanwhile a force of eighty Paras landed about five hundred metres from "Dengue" and began their advance. A disoriented Boavida fled mistakenly into the Para force and suddenly found himself next to a Para on the edge of the encampment. There was a short scuffle between the two, and the Para's pistol fired at point blank range, killing the doctor instantly.[19]

The Paras thoroughly searched the camp and found much matériel of all types that included bathing suits, excellent cameras, and valuable documents – all of which was either destroyed or loaded into helicopters. The Para commander noted the size and quality of the camp with its elaborate kitchen designed to meet the needs of the assembly and the important enemy leadership meeting. There was also a political indoctrination centre, a parade, and some forty huts, all of which were destroyed. The interlocking modular defensive networks surrounding the camp were oriented toward a conventional ground attack and not to an aerial envelopment, hence the success of the Paras. They were impressive in their careful camouflage and illustrated the extraordinary importance of "Dengue" as a primary MPLA command post in the east.[20]

NINDA

The operation, performed in the late 1960s from Ninda by CCP 2 and described by Lieutenant Joaquim Mensurado, targeted a small MPLA column making its way into the ZML and establishing an encampment located some distance from the Para base in difficult terrain. The choice of this location meant that any ground approach would be protracted for the Portuguese and thus they would forfeit the key element of surprise and any hope of success. The Paras in a heli-borne assault were the answer. Helicopters served to shorten the time forces took to travel such distances and thus introduce the opportunity for shock. With luck, this would work for the Paras of CCP 2.[21]

As the tropical dawn approached on the morning of the operation, the helos were ready with their blades turning in a constant rhythm. The Paras, fully briefed and preflighted, ran to the waiting aircraft with their bodies bent and heads lowered to avoid the blades above. With all aboard, the helos lifted off in sequence, each creating an enormous swirl of dust. Once airborne, the Paras in the half-light scrutinised the horizon through the curved windshield in search of life in the immense savanna ahead of them. For more than an hour the helos flew over scrub trees that dotted the inhospitable expanse, when at last they spotted a small copse of trees – the target. The helos approached the edge of this wood to hover and deposit the Paras. By all indications this isolated copse was the correct choice, as it provided the only opportunity for concealment on the horizon.[22]

When the Paras jumped the one-metre distance to the ground in disembarking and began to run as one, the force split into two teams side by side and partially surrounded the wood. It was difficult to see its interior, but as the Paras advanced, they encountered a group of small huts well hidden in the dense thicket. The first team opened fire on some insurgents who were caught by surprise and fled in various directions. The team, well trained and disciplined, pursued the enemy to the middle of the camp and investigated hut after hut with an elevated proficiency and professionalism. The enemy, now in flight, returned fire wildly. The team on the southern flank wounded two and killed another insurgent. The team on the northern flank encountered some resistance, and forced the enemy to flee into the fire of the other team, killing two insurgents.[23]

The landing had been well organised and brilliantly executed as dawn broke. It completely surprised the enemy and denied him adequate reaction time. By every indication he was still in bed sleeping, tired after a long march with a heavy pack across the sandy ground of eastern Angola. Fortunately the Paras suffered no mishaps. When it was over, the Paras shared their relief and joy in the midst of the miniscule encampment of six huts. These were little more than low shelters. The complete surprise of the enemy was the clear reason for success. The insurgents who escaped had a long road to safety with few places to hide and would not likely survive for long.[24] This type of operation was repeated time and time again from Ninda and was characteristic of Para activity along the Route of the Cuando.

LOOKING BACK

War in the east had benefitted from the earlier learning period between 1961 and 1969 in addressing the enemy in the north. During the opening enemy moves in the east, specific task forces were assembled to address targeted incursions and threats as stopgap measures. The overall effort at the time remained the north, but when proselytisation of the eastern population arose alarmingly in 1968 and the east required attention and resources, it received them. Portugal then proceeded to define the battlefield and develop a strategy of containment and attrition that addressed the vast open spaces of the east with its limited forces. Integral to the solution were the highly mobile groups of elite troops employed as hunter-killer forces, and airpower and the Paras were keys to this approach and its success. The enemy's intentions and behaviour became easily predictable, and this predictability made him highly vulnerable to airmobile forces. Arrival of the heavy SA-330 Puma helicopters in 1970 with their increased carrying capacity made an enormous difference in Para mobility and lethality. There developed a perfect resonance between the helicopter pilots and the Paras, and the melding of intelligence and this aviation-ground force team enabled the very effective pursuit and destruction of enemy columns. The assiduous practice of this concept through a series of seasonal campaigns produced tactical teams of devastating capability in a difficult physical environment that destroyed the enemy. By 1972 the Paras had shifted their attention back to the North, and the commandos had taken the lead in the East, as the Paras implemented their newly specialised tracking teams in destroying the enemy columns and bases remaining in the North.

By October 1973, UPA/FNLA and MPLA forces in the ZML were done. For the UPA/FNLA the crisis was complete. For the MPLA, it was reduced to sneaking across the border from its bases in Zambia and planting mines along the frontier roads. Its actions along the border were violent and short in both duration and penetration. The notion here was to strike a blow against the Portuguese that would open the way for a column to penetrate inland. This never worked.

For the Portuguese, there had been a profound revolution in their strategic and tactical concepts, and in one of the rare moments in history, the guerrilla was conquered. More importantly, however, was the mobilisation of the population, with funding support, to effect an economic recovery that led to indispensable social stabilisation.[25]

In an appraisal of the situation by Brigadier Hélio Felgas, he reported that by the beginning of April 1974 there was no contact between Portuguese forces and the insurgent groups of any of the nationalist organisations. By the end of April the southeast of Angola was calm, and insurgent activity was practically non-existent.[26]

The population sought to escape control of the MPLA and the other nationalist movements and nowhere was this more evident than in the explosion of education during the war in Angola.[27] By the 1970s under the protection of the security umbrella one saw daily thousands of children in their white smocks walking to school. The undisputed statistics prove this learning expansion. A decade previously such a phenomena would have been hard to imagine.[28] Portugal's victory permitted the people to envision a future more worthy and different from the tragedy that was to follow.

CHAPTER 6
SECURING THE NORTH OF ANGOLA

The north of Angola had presented a problem for Portuguese forces since the beginning in 1961, as its remoteness and difficult terrain mantled with luxuriant growth presented a perfect place for easy insurgent concealment. Further it was a magnet for insurgents, as it represented the most direct route from the Congo frontier to Luanda, the perceived Angolan centre of gravity for the Portuguese. The apparent short distance on a map was an illusion, however, as the route itself was a grave challenge. The general mode of insurgent operation was to establish base camps hidden in the fastness of the mountainous jungle known as the Dembos Forest with the intent of mounting operations against Portuguese forces that would lead to a final assault on Luanda. However, once they had reached the Dembos, they could not so easily mount offensives from their redoubts, as the Portuguese could limit the enemy to his fastness. The answer to routing him from his internal sanctuary was the prevention of his reinforcement. This meant intercepting his replenishment columns from the Congo bringing supplies and fighters. Again, in an attrition strategy, if the redoubts were isolated,

North of Angola Showing the UCTI Area and the M'Bridge River Basin. (*Map by the author*)

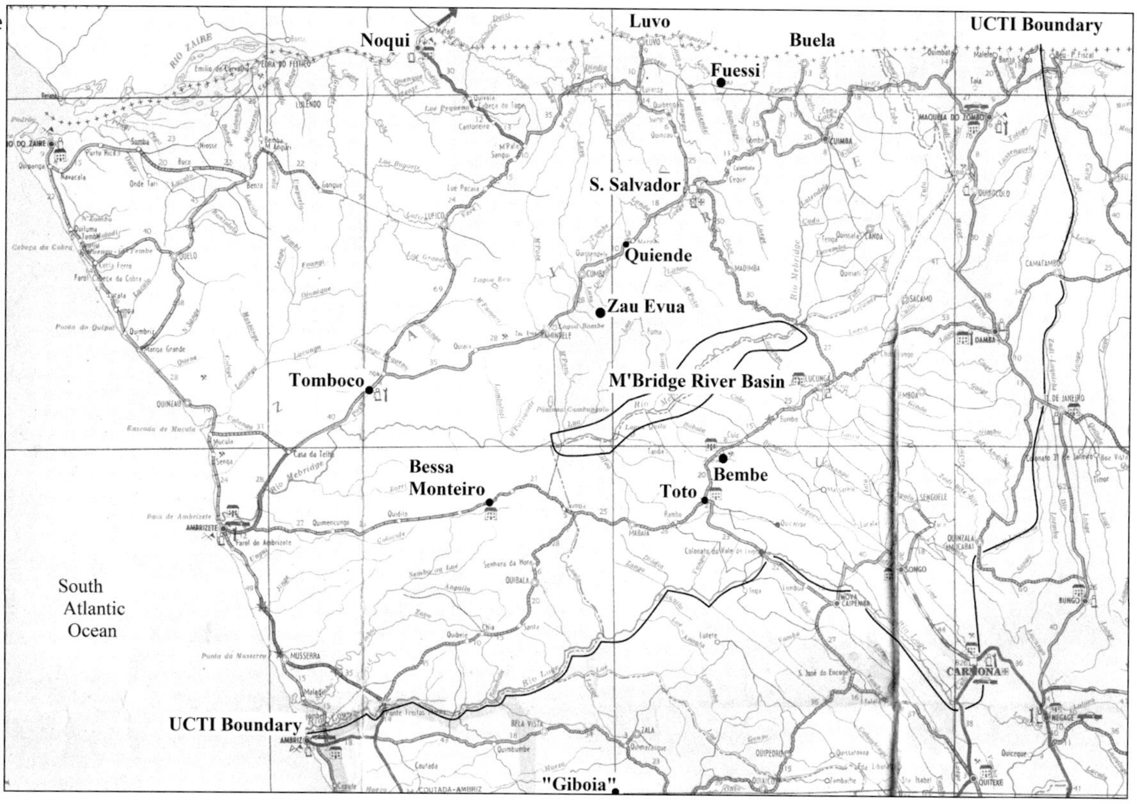

the insurgents would become increasingly a besieged and starving lot. This isolation was achieved through the use of specialised airmobile teams of Paras that were more agile, powerful, and persistent than the insurgent reinforcement columns and could locate and destroy them, even as they hid in difficult, indeed forbidding, terrain. These Portuguese units were conceived and born in mid-1972 and from this point onward militarily the days of the enemy in the north were numbered. The Paras, having operated in the east since 1967, now brought their skills to the north again.

ESTABLISHING THE UTCI

Infiltration of enemy units into the north of Angola from what by 1972 was known as the Republic of Zaire seemed to be an endless security problem that demanded a solution. For instance, in one of the few effective reappearances of UPA/FNLA insurgents in the Dembos area, a new column appeared in March 1971 and established a base camp named José Dias in honour of one of its luminaries. This camp was well defended and quickly became the source of much mischief. *Flechas,* the PIDE/DGS tracking and intelligence gathering troops, operating in the area on 7 March, identified the encampment at coordinates 08°49' South – 013°58' East and laid plans to assault it the next day.[1] At about 0430 hours just prior to dawn, when the *flechas* were encircling the headquarters, they were taken under fire by the insurgents. In the ensuing action, the *flechas* rescued prisoners consisting of two men, six women, and eleven children, and took a *canhangulo,* a homemade firearm. In debriefing the rescued group, the *flechas* learned that the insurgents maintained a rigorous lookout, as every evening the area was subject to aerial reconnaissance, and this surveillance made them very nervous.[2] Now pinpointed, further prosecution of the enemy camp was given over to heavier forces. This was a frustrating development, as the insurgents, once in place within the Dembos, were nearly impossible to dislodge.

In July of 1972, after a year of increasing insurgent presence, the Commander of the Angolan Air Region, General Rui Bras de Oliveira, and his chief of staff, Major Aurélio Benito Abeixo Corbal, assembled what they hoped would become a solution to this insidious infiltration.[3] The two officers sought to utilise the capabilities of Squadron 94, the *Moscas* (Flies), with its Alouette III and Puma helicopters based at Luanda and BCP 21 to form heli-borne teams founded on a select group of Paras with an as yet unperfected specialisation in tracking. These were to be embarked in helicopters for mobility and use their skills to identify suspicious activity on trails from the air. If the situation required a closer look, they could then be inserted onto the trail in question. The tactical intelligence so developed was to be followed by a powerful heli-borne team to destroy the insurgents. This team with its methodology was named the Tactical Counter-Infiltration Unit (*Unidade Táctica de Contra Infiltração* or UTCI).[4]

The detection of trails created by travelling groups and the interpretation of tracking intelligence in terms of the type of people, their direction, speed, and loads carried tended to be an inexact science based on tracker judgment and acquired experience in the bush. One almost had to be born into it. Moreover, its application in the modern military environment had been largely displaced by advances in technology, and hence it was somewhat of a lost art.[5] The war of the guerrilla, however, with its "hide and seek" nature required that this ancient skill be reacquired, and Portugal made great investments to do so. Both Rhodesia and South Africa were faced with the identical problem of tracking insurgent incursions and had acquired specially trained troops with experience in this skill. Portugal reviewed the results of its neighbours and was impressed. It was thus decided to develop this capability within the elite forces, and accordingly, arrangements were made to begin.[6]

The first course for trackers was held at the headquarters of the commandos in Luanda, and the paratroops attended. It was conducted by veteran Rhodesian officer and sergeant trackers over a three-month period. During the course the Rhodesians issued ten invitations to the most promising students, four to paratroopers and six to commandos, to attend the practical tracking course in

Typical Alouette III echelon. (*Source Archivo Histórico da Força Aérea*)

Paras boarding Puma helicopters. (*Source Archivo Histórico da Força Aérea*)

Rhodesia. Upon the return of these students, they constituted the nucleus of tracking capability in Angola and were responsible for preparing a course at Belas for officers and sergeants that began in July 1973.[7] The course had both a theoretical and practical side. The first taught the techniques of tracking and methodology of interpreting the signs of the trails, such as the number of people passing on it, the age of the signs, the weight of the travellers, and the difference between the fighters and the porters. The second was a practical application. The course ran continuously, and its students were immediately integrated into front line units as both aerial and terrain trackers. The immediate results were very positive and clearly reinforced the decision to invest in this capability. As the course matured, other army units were able to send personnel for training. The third course was held in Luso and aimed at the locally recruited forces in the east.[8]

The UCTI initially was composed of two echelons. The first had two Alouette IIIs, one a transport with two trackers and the other a gunship for their protection. The second echelon was composed of a Puma, which transported fifteen Paras, a gunship, and a Noratlas with three additional combat groups. Once the first echelon located the column, the second swooped down on the unsuspecting insurgents and destroyed them. The entire force acted only on intelligence that confirmed the enemy had crossed the border with Zaire in force. The UCTI was forward-based at the manoeuvre airfield at Toto, which was about eighty miles from the northern border in the District of Uíge.[9]

(Insert nearby Photo 6.1: T

After about a year of these "reconnaissance-in-force" actions and their refinement, Bras de Oliveira issued a formal document defining and regulating these missions and providing guidelines for those who performed them. He also established a permanent command at Toto to run them: the Special Command for Counter-Infiltration (*Comando Especial de Contra Infiltração* or CECI). This command operated in a zone defined by:

- To the north, the frontier with Zaire,
- To the east, the Zadi and the Zadi-Luquiche Rivers to their source just north of Carmona,
- To the south, the Loge River from the Vale do Loge at Carmona to the Atlantic Ocean, and
- To the west, the Atlantic Ocean.

The area where the infiltrating insurgents were most vulnerable – the one presenting the greatest obstacle to their progress southward – was the M'Bridge River Basin. Their goal was to reach the forest region northeast of Luanda, and their route from the Zairian border directly south to it took them through this area. It was perfect terrain for them, as it was remote and sparsely populated. For the UCTI this basin midway along the course of the M'Bridge River was a "happy hunting ground," as it was here that interception operations were the most fruitful.[10]

This formalisation also restructured the forces available to CECI, and they were now:

- An Air Group, designated the "Royal Falcon," of an Alouette III gunship and two Alouette III transports. These were supported by the airbases at Luanda and Negage.
- A permanent detachment of a combat group of twenty Paras, including trackers and sappers, furnished by the Paratroop Battalion in Belas, south of Luanda.

It was still the job of the first echelon to develop and interpret the tracking intelligence for an intercept mission, but now there were additional trackers in a second Alouette III to allow leapfrog tactics in developing the picture. Troop numbers and aircraft for the second echelon, which still included a combat group of twenty Paras, were to be tailored to developments and kept as a reserve on alert. Depending on what the interception required, additional troops or air support must be arranged and, in the judgment of the CECI, must be a force most likely to be effective.

INTERCEPTION OPERATIONS

The first FAP intercept operations were prompted by intelligence from tracking reconnaissance gathered in late 1971 and early 1972 during the height of the rainy season, when the rivers were swollen and incursion columns were experiencing difficult progress southward from Zaire. Their slow pace and extended presence in areas of vulnerability, such as river crossings, provided an opportunity for discovery. The FAP tracking effort gradually intensified, and as it did so, the technique of both the Alouette III pilots and the Para trackers improved measurably. In fact, the coordination between the two, as each came to appreciate the role of the other, became very close. The most fruitful area for interception and tracking – and thus employing the teams – was the intersection between a north-south line from São Salvador to Toto and the M'Bridge River, which ran from east to west. It was a natural obstacle to insurgent columns and forced them to pause and regroup for a crossing. Further, the river could only be crossed at certain points, particularly in the rainy season, so the regroupings predictably occurred at these locations and forced the enemy to mass and reveal himself. Notwithstanding this, even when the enemy did arrange to cross the M'Bridge, and the FAP knew his intention, the intercept was never certain.[11]

Within this operational context, one of the first truly successful intercepts occurred over the last days of 1972 and the first ones of

1973, again during the rainy season, to the north of the M'Bridge and east of the village of Zau Évua, headquarters of an army battalion that was part of the quadrille defence system. The enemy force was a supply column consisting of between seventy and eighty elements. Its progress was detected and followed by tracker teams operating from two Alouette IIIs working north to south between São Salvador and Quiende. As the reconnaissance progressed, the trackers came closer and closer to the column and just before the intercept spent two days undetected overlooking the locale where the column bivouacked for two nights.[12]

When the commander of the Air Group had fixed the column, he activated his second echelon composed of two Pumas, each carrying a combat group of fifteen Paras and each escorted by a gunship. Further, the reserve of three additional Para combat groups were loaded onto a Noratlas and departed Luanda for the area.[13]

The Pumas flew a nap-of-the-earth profile directly from Toto to the target area and deposited the Paras on the terrain around the enemy's trail, a move that allowed them to comb the area as efficiently as possible in an attempt to gain contact. Three of the Paras entered an uneven bit of terrain made so by the presence of a stream covered by very dense vegetation, and one of them suddenly found himself in the midst of the enemy in hiding. He quietly and quickly retreated and signalled for the gunship to rake the tuft of foliage. Several bursts of fire followed. The Paras were fortunate in not being hit, but the fire of the gunship caused the enemy to flee into the open. The gunship, now exhausted of ammunition, departed for Zau Évua to rearm, while another gunship was inbound. As soon as the two gunships were on station, they raked the areas where the enemy had sought refuge. The Paras rounded up the survivors and accounted for the entire column. Aside from the killed and captured enemy, the Paras found great quantities of light arms, anti-personnel and anti-vehicle mines, and supplies.[14]

Alouette III gunship being readied for a mission. (*Source Archivo Histórico da Força Aérea*)

Noratlas transport aircraft at an improvised airfield. (*Source Archivo Histórico da Força Aérea*)

THE KEY: INTELLIGENCE

The key to an insurgent intercept was a timely knowledge of the time and place that he intended to cross the frontier. Intelligence on his intentions was gathered from informers who had infiltrated the insurgent centres in the Zairian sanctuary or from the interrogation of prisoners. Once a planned incursion was anticipated, the FAP pilots and trackers were launched and commenced searching for signs of the column. There was, however, often a great lag in time between the decision to form a column by the insurgent leadership and its actual appearance in the north of Angola. This delay meant that intelligence, while accurate, suffered from a certain operational friction within the insurgent movement in simply getting things done. There generally was little sense of urgency, or even if there was, organising and launching a column generally proved time consuming. Eventually though, as the column was launched and progressed, it generated clues that advertised its presence when it finally crossed the border and proceeded along its route. As the column left signs, FAP aerial reconnaissance and the tracking teams began to pinpoint its location and define its movement. This ultimately led to the destruction of the large majority of enemy columns entering Angola from the north, and from the time that the UTCI tracking units were initiated in mid-1972, insurgent columns were destroyed with disturbing regularity for the enemy. His bases began dying, and his ability to maintain them at any level of readiness was severely weakened. This translated into an inability to conduct operations, and within the north insurgent bases struggled simply to survive.[15]

It is worth describing two further cases to illustrate these intercept operations, and in the first we begin with Paulo Panda, who was a UPA/FNLA insurgent commander with a great deal of experience leading groups infiltrating from Zaire. In early 1973 he commanded a column destined to resupply the UPA/FNLA base of "Gibóia" (Boa Constrictor), which lay to the northeast of Luanda and was responsible for the subversion of the coastal villages of Ambriz, Capulo, Barra do Dande, and Tabi. Several days after entering Angolan territory, he was overflown by a number of Dornier reconnaissance flights originating from Toto, as they monitored the traditional trails of likely columns. Panda was forced to proceed cautiously, and this slowed his progress. Further, Panda became sick, and this necessitated his remaining behind. Without its leader, the column began to make mistakes and revealed itself. It took only a day before it was attacked by three combat groups of Paras (about sixty troops) supported by two gunships. The first attack was made by a single combat group that was dropped at the rear of the column, and this forced the insurgents and porters to disperse and abandon great quantities of matériel. Meanwhile, the second combat group in a Puma was dropped in front of the column blocking the direction of flight. Surrounded and confronted, the insurgents and porters became disoriented and attempted to flee in all directions. Three were killed, three captured, and an undetermined number wounded. The third combat group landed and helped to "fine comb" the area. This proved very difficult, as the terrain was highly irregular with escarpments and ravines, all with dense vegetation. It was likely that the insurgents dispersed in groups of two or three and hid until the Paras left.[16]

A Douglas B-26 Invader parked on the ramp at Luanda with its heat-diffusing green coating livery and the absence of identifying markings. The six .50-calibre machineguns in its nose could fire explosive projectiles. (*Source Archivo Histórico da Força Aérea*)

Panda was ultimately captured and in captivity furnished intelligence on a column that had entered Angola shortly after his in the area of Noqui in the spring of 1973 and was composed of insurgents escorting a large group of heavily laden porters. It represented an excellent target for the UTCI, which quickly identified the trail used by the large group.[17] The trail was followed across the Tomboco-São Salvador road, and the trackers estimated that they were four to five days behind the column. From this point the FAP tracking teams began their work using the usual two Alouette IIIs as transport and a gunship for protection. The trackers followed the trail some kilometres to the south along the Quiende River, which ran south to north through Quiende, and entered an area of dense foliage where the track became difficult to follow. By mid-afternoon they were joined by a combat group of Paras who arrived in two Pumas. The trackers followed the trail until the end of the afternoon. At about 1900 hours, when the light began to fade, they saw that the track skirted a small thicket, entered a larger one, and disappeared into its interior where there were footprints in all directions. Because the light was fading quickly and quite dim, it was difficult to know which direction the column had taken. After a short time another trail was detected that entered a thicket opposite the one under investigation. This reversal was a normal precautionary procedure designed to make detection difficult just as the column was preparing to bivouac overnight. A quick check of the immediate area confirmed that the column had remained overnight there recently, as the Paras found a spade and a canteen next to extinguished campfires. There were three of these campsites about thirty metres apart and within each the grass was pressed flat from sleeping porters and insurgents. The remains of animal skins were also evident, but there was little else of note. Interestingly there was also a lookout post, a small detached area where sentries had stood watch to protect the principal group and make certain that its leaders were not surprised while sleeping. In consideration of the lateness of the day and the impossibility of making further progress, the Para commander decided to bivouac nearby.[18]

The next day at 0500 the tracking was begun anew and followed to a point where the trail left the grass and headed west. It then inflected north to cross the Quiende River and wound along its left (east) bank where another overnight campsite was discovered not far from the previous one. This one was different, however, in that it extended along the riverbank with numerous hot fire sites, some still burning. After a quick reconnaissance of the campsite, the Paras continued their advance to the south between two trails that ran parallel and close to each other. By 0730 the trackers had closed to within 300 metres of the enemy, whose trail exited a small thicket, proceeded across a small clearing, and entered major vegetation. This was certainly the present location of the enemy.[19]

After the Paras informed their command post, they began a cautious approach with two sections moving in parallel, one taking up a position on the left edge of the thicket without detection and the other moving around the thicket to the right about eighty metres from the target, a position that permitted a vantage for either defence or attack. The approach of the Paras and the nearness of the gunships signalled the beginning of the assault. As the Paras on the left began to fire and advance in a "hammer and anvil" tactic, the enemy reacted with wild fire from automatic weapons and sought to abandon his position as quickly as possible. The gunships overflew the enemy position and made his movement very difficult. In the disorderly flight, porters and insurgents alike abandoned their loads and attempted to disappear into the high grass. Simultaneously the section on the right, which was some distance away, unleashed its fire. The heli-transported reserve now arrived and assumed the just-vacated position on the left. The gunships raked the thicket in front of the Paras as they advanced. As the sections of Paras worked their way through the thicket, the enemy fled in all directions. By 1130 the reserve was combing the battleground and found signs of the explosive projectiles from the gunship cannons, the remains of bloody clothes, and many abandoned loads. These largely consisted of RPGs and automatic weapons, hand grenades, anti-personnel and anti-vehicle mines, munitions and fuses.[20] No figures were offered on the number of enemy killed, wounded, or captured.

The second example occurred on 3 July 1974, three months after the April revolution, which had little immediate influence on the fighting in Africa. On this late date the UTCI led by Captain Fidalgo was composed of two Alouette III transports with trackers and a gunship and deployed to an area northeast of Quiende and west of São Salvador. The UTCI was acting on intelligence that had identified a border crossing by insurgents to the west of Luvo.[21]

This small search force looked for several days without success and eventually moved further west where earlier infiltrators had passed. Finally the trackers located a recently used trail along which a group of more than a hundred infiltrators had passed two to three days earlier. Pursuit of the column proceeded rapidly, as the trackers could now follow the trail from the air and needed to land only occasionally to confirm signs on the ground and refine their information. These quick glances allowed the two Alouette IIIs to leapfrog one another and move quickly to contact with the enemy. By the end of the day there was sufficient knowledge to move an intercept force into position, and the Alouette IIIs returned to Toto to prepare for pursuit the following day.[22] Meanwhile, notice was given to the Paras to be prepared for an intercept.

On 4 July before dawn the tracker force of three Alouette IIIs launched from Toto and flew to the point where the search had been broken the preceding evening. Here there were the remains of fires and other signs of a recently abandoned bivouac. This new information was relayed to Luanda and reinforcements were prepared. There were two Pumas, a company of Paras, and two B-26 Invaders armed with fragmentation bombs. This ordnance was aimed at softening the column before the Paras were inserted.[23]

The two Pumas flew to Toto each with a combat group of Paras aboard to preposition for the operation. Meanwhile, Fidalgo was flying over the trail scouting for an appropriate landing zone for the Paras when, as he skirted a small elevation in the terrain next to a thicket, he saw in the middle of the trail an insurgent holding a rifle and immobilised, indeed hypnotised, by the sight of the helicopter. Fidalgo reacted immediately and flew low over the enemy, who jumped aside to avoid being "hit" by the helicopter and then quickly disappeared into the bush. Clearly the column was nearby, and it was important to act rapidly. While the gunship continued to circle the thicket, Fidalgo requested B-26 fire support and the Pumas with their combat groups. The B-26s raked the site with their bombs and machineguns and were followed by the Pumas. The landing zone was on the north rim of the dense vegetation, and the landed Paras quickly moved south into the area still smouldering from the passes by the B-26s. The Paras encountered no resistance and observed a number of bodies left by the staffing.

The Paras were commanded by Lieutenant Colonel Almendra, who on reconnoitring the area from the air decided to call for a second insertion of two combat groups on the far side of the thicket with the intention of capturing the remaining elements of the column who sought to escape in that direction. However, as his plan was being executed, the Alouette III gunship departed for Bessa Monteiro to refuel and rearm, and this left the ground troops without close air support.[24]

Meanwhile, on the ground the Paras returned to the south rim and re-entered the thicket, where they found no insurgents. As they emerged on the other side, they found that the fleeing insurgents had set fire to the grass. It now burned with great ferocity and forced the Paras to detour around the flames. This move put them in an unfavourable position, and the enemy, taking advantage, opened fire with automatic weapons and grenade launchers and wounded two Paras. Fidalgo flying his Alouette III had no arms and could only guide the Para attack. Suddenly the enemy fire practically ceased.[25]

During this moment a vulnerable Alouette III landed to evacuate the two wounded without the protection of the gunship that was still refuelling. An urgent and unprotected evacuation in combat was always worrisome, and now as the wounded were being loaded as quickly as possible, a blast of machinegun fire hit the two wounded and aggravated their condition. The helicopter was also hit but

A typical MEDEVAC under combat conditions. (*Source Archivo Histórico da Força Aérea*)

executed a lift-off away from the source of the fire and, skimming the treetops, headed for Toto.[26]

Sometime later after an intense search for the enemy, the Paras agreed that as night approached, they would manoeuvre toward an elevation about 300 metres from the thicket and establish a defensive perimeter for the night bivouac. Before doing so, however, the Paras asked the Alouette IIIs to inspect the site from the air after again refuelling in Bessa Monteiro. While there, Fidalgo's helicopter refused to start following its refuelling, and he changed places with the gunship pilot to return to the scene of the action. On doing so, he was told that the enemy was now located along a small stream that wound through the thicket. Positioning the gunship to rake the banks of the stream, the gunner fired into what was a largely obscured or only partially visible target. After a few long bursts from the cannon, the enemy returned fire with his light arms from the small openings in the dense vegetation.[27] The return fire hit the gunship in several places and wounded the gunner in his right leg. Fidalgo immediately broke contact and turned towards Toto, which was a twenty- to thirty-minute flight. The damage to the helicopter was minor, but the gunner had lost much blood and made a tourniquet from an old, oily rag that he had found in the helicopter to stem the flow. Fidalgo landed next to the Noratlas that was evacuating the two wounded Paras and loaded his gunner on board with them.[28]

The following morning, the Paras now with the support of two gunships made a final attack on the enemy position. Enemy elements fled in part, while some porters were captured or simply surrendered exhausted. The Paras found a great amount of supplies, some automatic weapons, a large quantity of ammunition, and many anti-personnel and anti-vehicle mines.[29]

It is certainly possible to describe many more UCTI operations that illustrate the effectiveness of its mixed air-land components. The fine tuning of UCTI allowed it to prevail over the enemy in the north and to choke his supply lines to the point that he became virtually impotent.[30]

SUCCESS OF CONSTANT PRESSURE

In June 1973, a group of native trackers known as *flechas* detected and followed the tracks of a group of twenty-five insurgents who when surprised fled, abandoning some salt and bananas and parts of Claymore mines.[31] This was a group attempting to resupply "Gibóia," a UPA/FNLA base that was subsisting exclusively on meat from hunting, a situation similar to that of "Tigre" (Tiger) in the area of Tabi, a small coastal village about forty miles north of Luanda and

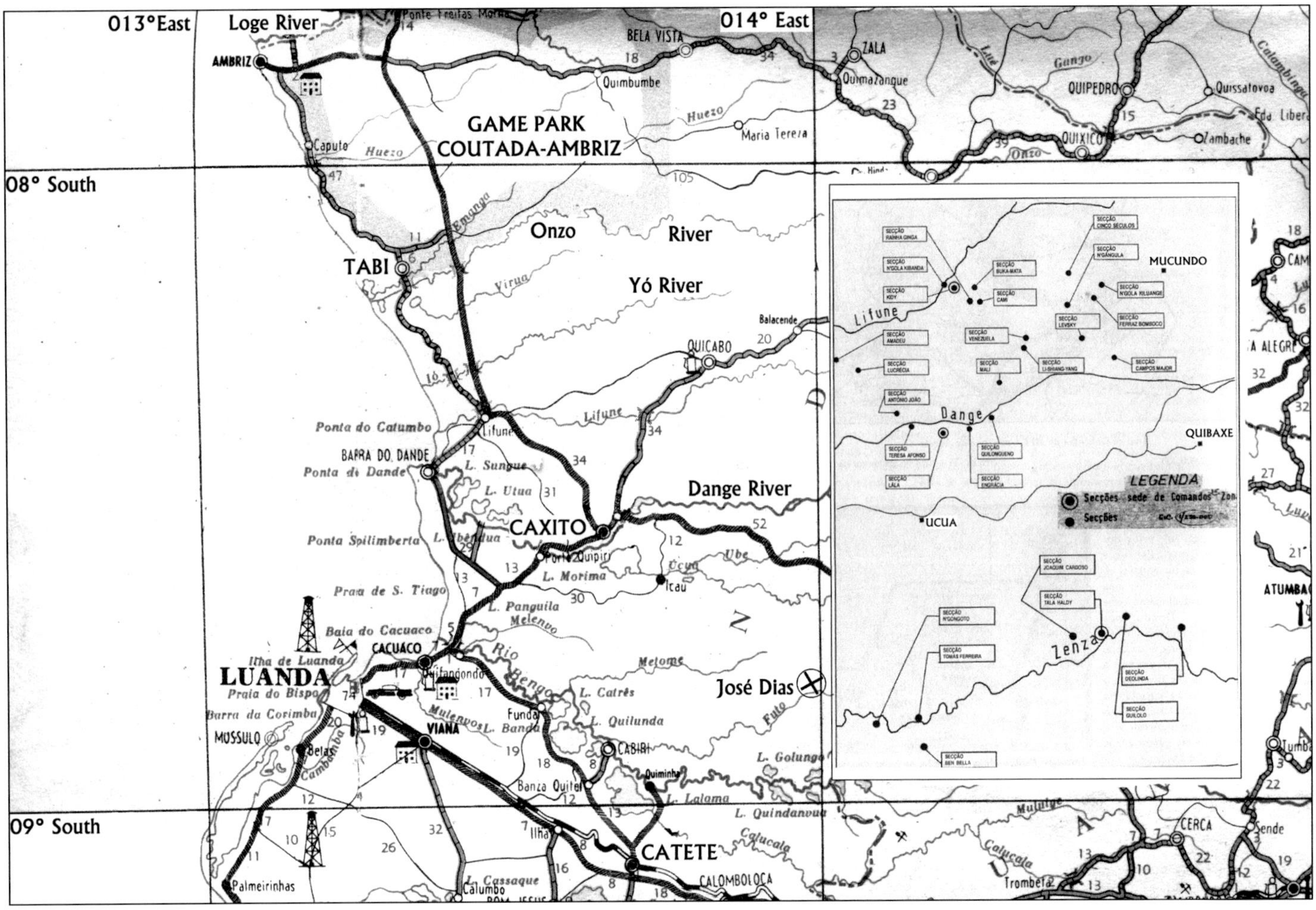

Enemy encampments in the Dembos Forest region, 1970–1973 (*Source the author*) with MPLA Base Locations, Dembos Region inserted (*Map by the Comissão para Estudo das Campanhas de África*)

An Alouette III discharging its five Paras. (*Source Archivo Histórico da Força Aérea*)

bordering the game park Coutada-Ambriz. Intelligence reported symptoms of indiscipline, disorganisation, and demoralisation among the UPA/FNLA troops operating in the area between the Loge and Onzo Rivers, which define the northern and southern boundaries of the Coutada-Ambriz. Captured documents indicated that a total of 667 "military" personnel had returned to the Congo since December 1971 and were a part of the clandestine dissident activity in the UPA/FNLA camp at Kinkuzu. Apparently in this case there was a complete failure of the political commissars to maintain troop loyalty to the Holden Roberto regime.[32]

Again a week later between 10 and 13 July, These several actions involved insurgents from "Tigre," whose members were surviving like nomads and had been dispersed as a result of relentless pursuit. The company commander Paulo Sebastião Domingos, whose nom-de-guerre was *São Paulo*, was fleeing and hiding in the bush with his fellow insurgent Mateus Dias Ideia. They were now using their weapons and precious little remaining ammunition to survive by hunting game rather than fighting.[33]

Insurgents belonging to the MPLA base "Ben Bella," like many others, were living as nomads. The group was surviving next to the base "Tomás Ferreira," which had been destroyed earlier on 17 June.[34] Most of the insurgent troops had returned to Zaire, and those remaining were psychologically spent from the relentless pressure of Portuguese forces. Base after base had been dissolved, and those responsible ordered the remaining to live near native villages for support. This facilitated their capture and the rescue of those elements of the population forced to support them.[35]

In the north of Angola by the end of the war, both the UPA/FNLA and the MPLA were forces strangled, exhausted, and confined to a completely circumscribed area in the fastness of the Dembos. Both were isolated, starving, only partially armed, and desperate. The Dembos was difficult for anyone because of its impossible terrain, and in essence hiding there, as the enemy forces were doing, was neutralising oneself as a threat.

The development and perfection of the UTCI had reduced the enemy cadres to a state of simple survival in the depths of the Dembos. Columns attempting to travel the 150 miles from the northern frontier to this sanctuary faced an alerted and capable opponent, one with experienced and proficient trackers who used helicopters to follow the trail at a pace far faster than the column could advance. The trackers and helicopters were able to employ stealth and remain undetected by the column until the UTCI was ready to pounce. The column had little warning that it was being targeted, and when it was surrounded and cornered, there was little choice but to abandon the supply loads and weapons to permit unencumbered flight. Members of the broken column, if not killed or captured, became refugees in an unfamiliar land, easily identifiable and ultimately captured. Some, of course, gained their destination base or returned to Zaire, but those captured talked readily and easily and revealed what they knew. The intelligence gathered from the prisoners insured the destruction of subsequent columns and surviving bases. New columns were regularly broken and surviving bases reduced to ineffectiveness as they withered. The UTCI was indeed a powerful and effective counterinsurgency tool.

CHAPTER 7
TRAGEDY

For thirteen years Portugal was confronted by an international community manifestly hostile to its presence in Africa and committed to oppose it by all means available. Ignored in this hostility were the centuries of Portuguese presence in these African regions and the Portuguese efforts to bring to them advances in education, health care, and economic prosperity. In 1961 Portugal found itself in a fight to retain its African possessions that extended from the Atlantic to the Indian Ocean, to both sides of the equator, and to thousands of square miles of vast and difficult terrain. This campaign represented one of the largest combat fronts in modern history. The logistics of training, deploying, and supplying forces to fight on such an expansive battlefield was staggering. The paratrooper units, scattered across the mountains, savannas, jungles, and forests of Africa, enduring the hardships of isolation in the bush and the remoteness of the battlefields, fought a noble action – one that is today little remembered. For them this was a war not lost on the field of battle but in the haplessness of flawed political leadership.

The Paras of 1CCP lower the Portuguese flag for the last time at Fortaleza do São Miguel in Luanda just prior to their departure on 10 November 1975. (*Source Museu das Pára-quedistas*)

The Paras, born under the clear vision and understanding of Kalúza de Arriaga that there was an important place for such troops in counterinsurgency, earned a valuable role in the Portuguese Air Force. Arriaga had witnessed the French and Americans develop airmobile forces and saw the same need in Portuguese Africa. It was he who gave them the best equipment and training of any Portuguese force at the time and who had the vision to mate them with the helicopter so that they could move in numbers, and surprise and overwhelm the enemy on the African battlefield. Such shock troops always paid a price in casualties. A total of 160 Paras gave their lives over the thirteen years of war in Africa, and their heroism was remarkable for such a small force of about 1,900 men. In 1968 BCP 12 was decorated with the Cruz de Guerra, first class. The next year BCP 31 also received the same award. In 1973 BCP 21 received the Gold Medal for Military Valour with Palm. In 1985, a decade after decolonisation, when their sacrifice and contribution was more fully understood and appreciated, the new Parachute Corps was made an Honorary Member of the Order of the Tower and Sword, Portugal's highest award for valour.

Paratroopers killed in Action

Unit	Killed in Action	Officers	Sergeants	Soldiers
BCP 12	56	3	6	47
BCP 21	47	5	9	33
BCP 31	39	2	6	31
BCP 32	18		2	16
Total	160	10	23	127

Source: Miguel Machado and António Carmo, Tropas Pára-quedistas: A História dos Boinas Verdes Portugueses, 1955–2003 [Paratroopers: The History of the Portuguese Green Berets, 1955–2003] (Lisbon: Prefácio, 2003), pp. 30–36.

In 1975 the four battalions in Africa and those in Tancos were combined into the Parachute Corps, and in 1994 in a reorganisation the Paras were made a part of the Portuguese Army in its Airmobile Troop Command, ending their nearly forty-year association with the FAP. In 2006 in yet another reorganisation they became the Rapid Reaction Brigade. Through all of these developments the Paras continued to be recognised by their distinctive Green Beret and still today are known as the "*Boinas Verdes.*"

NOTES

Chapter 1

1 Miguel António Gabriel da Silva Machado and António Eleutério Sucena do Carmo, "Tropas Pára-Quedistas Portuguesas" [Portuguese Paratroops], *Boina Verde* 158 (July–September 1991): p. 7.

2 Ibid.

3 The 8th Division of the Australian Army was formed in July 1940 in anticipation of World War Two and was a part of the Second Australian Imperial Force, the Australian contribution to the Allied war effort. The Division of 22,000 light infantrymen was divided into five forces, each to defend key terrain in the Asia-Pacific Theatre: Malaya, Singapore, Ambon, Rabaul, and Timor. In each case, the defending Australian force was overwhelmed by the Japanese, and all five components of the Division were destroyed as fighting forces by the end of February 1942. During this fighting over 2,500 men died in combat and another 7,500 died later as prisoners of war. This number of 10,000 represents two thirds of all deaths sustained by the Australian Army in the war.

4 The Australian Army did not possess any "special forces" units at the beginning of World War Two, however, in late 1940, the British offered assistance in building such a capacity. British thinking was that a series of independent companies be established and that the volunteers for these units be given advanced training so that they might support combined operations and other tasks, such as raids, demolition, sabotage, subversion, and organising civil resistance. The Australian Army began raising and training the 2/1st Independent Company in March 1941 modelled on the British Army Commando concept. Training was conducted at the 7th Infantry Training Centre, Guerrilla Warfare School, Wilson's Promontory, Victoria. By mid-1941, a total of three companies had been raised, and the second one, the 2/2nd Independent Company, was sent to Portuguese Timor in December 1941.

5 Ernest Chamberlain, *Forgotten Men: Timorese in Special Operations during World War II* (Point Lonsdale: Privately printed, 2010), p. 1.

6 Paul Cleary, *The Men Who Came Out of the Ground: A Gripping Account of Australia's First Commando Campaign, Timor, 1942* (Sydney: Hachette Australia, 2010), pp. 110–112.

7 Chamberlain, *Forgotten Men*, p. 1.

8 Luís António Martinho Grão, *História das Tropas Pára-Quedistas Portuguesas, Volume I, Tancos 1955–1961* [History of the Portuguese Paratroops, Volume I, Tancos 1955–1961] (Lisbon: Comando das Tropas Aerotransportadas, 1987), p. 55.

9 Machado and Carmo, "Tropas Pára-Quedistas Portuguesas," p. 7.

10 Ibid., p. 8.

11 Chamberlain, *Forgotten Men*, p. 61.

12 Machado and Carmo, "Tropas Pára-Quedistas Portuguesas," p. 8

13 Chamberlain, *Forgotten Men*, p. 15.

14 C.C.H. Wray, *Timor 1942: Australian Commandos at War with the Japanese* (Hutchinson, Australia: Hawthorn, 1987), pp. 166–167.

15 Chamberlain, *Forgotten Men*, p. 15.

16 Ibid., p. 22.

17 Cleary, *The Men Who Came Out of the Ground*, p. 299.

18 Chamberlain, *Forgotten Men*, p. 23.

19 Ibid., p. 63, fn. 401.

20 Ibid, p. 24.

21 Ibid., p. 25.

22 Ibid., p. 28.

23 Ibid.

24 Ibid., p. 30.

25 Ibid.

26 Cleary, *The Men Who Came Out of the Ground*, p. 311.

27 Ibid.

28 Ibid.

29 Ibid.

30 Ibid.

31 Ibid., p. 312.

32 Ibid., p. 326.

33 Machado and Carmo, "Tropas Pára-Quedistas Portuguesas": p. 9.

34 Ibid.

35 Ibid.

36 Ibid.

37 Grão, *História das Tropas Pára-Quedistas Portuguesas*, p. 36.

38 Machado and Carmo, "Tropas Pára-Quedistas Portuguesas": p. 13.

39 Ibid.

40 Ibid., p. 15.

41 Ibid., p. 26.

42 Ibid., p. 17.

43 Machado and Carmo, "Tropas Pára-Quedistas Portuguesas," p. 27.

44 Pedro Manuel Ferreira, "A missão que ficou por realizar 'Ibis' ou a pré-génese da instalacão da Força Aérea em Moçambique" [The Mission to Execute *Ibis* or the Groundwork for the Installation of the Air Force in Mozambique], *Mais Alto* 350 (July–August 2004): p. 22.

45 Ibid., p. 23.

46 Ibid.

47 Marcello Caetano, "Editorial," *O Mundo Português* [Portuguese World], 2 (1935): p. 218.

48 Peter Forbath, *The River Congo* (New York: Harper & Row, 1977), p. 384.

49 Adam Hochschild, *King Leopold's Ghost* (New York: Houghton Mifflin, 1998), p. 301.

50 Mike Hoar, *Congo Warriors* (London: Robert Hale, 1991), p. 10.

51 Hélio Augusto Esteves Felgas, *Relatório Pessoal Acerca do Congo Belga: Referente a Outubro 1959* [Personal Report Concerning the Belgian Congo: Referring to October 1959] (Carmona, Governor of the District of the Congo, 4 November 1959), Resende personal papers, Caixa 17, Proco 02, Arquivo Histórico de Força Aérea Portuguesa, Alfragide, p. 3.

52 Ibid.

53 Ibid.

54 Forbath, *River Congo,* p. 388.

55 Hoar, *Congo Warriors*, p. 12.

56 Forbath, *River Congo,* p. 390.

57 Hoar, *Congo Warriors*, p. 12.

58 Ibid., p. 13.

59 Ibid.

60 Felgas, *Relatório Pessoal Acerca do Congo Belga,* p. 3.

61 Grão, *História das Tropas Pára-Quedistas Portuguesas*, p. 235.

62 Machado and Carmo, "Tropas Pára-Quedistas Portuguesas": p. 31.

63 John A. Marcum, *The Angolan Revolution, Vol. I, The Anatomy of an Explosion (1950–1962)* (Cambridge, Mass.: MIT Press, 1969), 347–351. Marcum lists some fifty-nine groups affecting Angola alone beginning in the 1940s and either merging with one another or vanishing by 1962.

64 Malyn Newitt, *Portugal in Africa: The Last Hundred Years* (London: C. Hurst & Co., 1981), p. 190.

65 Douglas L. Wheeler and René Pélissier, *Angola* (London: Pall Mall Press, 1971), 167. The authors cite as an example the Congo district in 1960. For its 37,000 square miles it had fourteen *concelhos* (basic urban or semi-urban administrative unit) or *circunscrições* (basic rural administrative division) and thirty-seven posts, for an average of 725 square miles per administrative division. This presence would hardly be effective in controlling a frontier, as the posts would be dozens of miles apart. Large numbers of people could and did cross undetected.

66 Van der Waals, *Portugal's War in Angola 1961–1974*, p. 97. The author argues that Portuguese propaganda and social work among the refugees in Angola persuaded most of these displaced people to move into controlled

settlements. This development deprived ELNA of popular support. ELNA had concentrated on military action in a human desert and on preventing MPLA infiltration. It had neglected to indoctrinate, organise, and win recruits among refugees returning to Angola and thus missed an opportunity to undermine Portuguese authority. Consequently no ELNA internal political infrastructure was established in Angola. Portugal gained the upper hand and maintained superior momentum until 1974.

67 Ibid.

68 Adenekan, "Holden Roberto."

69 Ibid.

70 *Expresso* (Lisbon), 17 September 1974, p. 18.

71 Gleijeses, *Conflicting Millions*, p. 238.

72 António Lopes Pires Nunes, *Angola 1961: Da Baixa do Cassange a Nambuangongo* [Angola 1961: From Baixa do Cassange to Nambuangongo] (Lisbon: Prefácio, 2005), pp. 86–87.

73 Ibid.

74 Ibid.

75 Ibid.

76 René Pélissier, *Le Naufrage des Caravelles: Etudes sur la Fin de l'Empire Portuguais (1961–1975)* [The Shipwreck of the Caravels: Studies on the End of the Portuguese Empire] (Orgeval: Editions Pélissier, 1979, p. 147; Tomás George Conceição Silva, "The Portuguese Air Force in the African Wars of 1961–1974" in *Memories of Portugal's African Wars, 1961–1974* edited by John P. Cann (Quantico: Marine Corps University Foundation, 1998), p. 113; and Alexandra Correia, "O Dia da Barbárie" [The Day of Barbary], *Visão História* 12 (June 2011): p. 59.

77 Willem S. van der Waals, *Portugal's War in Angola 1961–1974* (Rivonia: Ashanti Publishing, 1993), p. 64.

78 Pélissier, *Naufrage des Caravelles,* p. 147.

79 Edgar Pereira da Costa Cardoso, *Presença da Força Aérea em Angola* [Presence of the Air Force in Angola] (Lisbon: Secretaria de Estado de Aeronáutica, 1963), p. 90.

80 Ibid., p. 91.

81 René Pélissier, *La Colonie du Minotaure: Nationalismes et Révoltes en Angola (1926–1961)* [The Colony of the Minotaur: Nationalist Movements and Revolts in Angola (1926–1961)] (Orgeval: Editions Pélissier, 1978, 657–660; and Willem S. van der Waals, *Portugal's War in Angola 1961–1974* (Rivonia: Ashanti Publishing, 1981), pp. 58–61.

82 Manuel Diogo Neto, "Acontecimentos no Norte de Angola" [Events in the North of Angola] *Mais Alto* 30 (June–July 1961): p. 9.

83 Ibid., p. 8.

Chapter 2

1 René Pélissier, *La Colonie du Minotaure, Nationalismes et Révoltes en Angola (1926–1961)* [Colony of the Minotaur, Nationalism and Revolts in Angola] (Orgeval: Editions Pélissier, 1978), p. 658.

2 John A. Marcum, *The Angolan Revolution: Volume I, The Anatomy of an Explosion (1950–1962)* (Cambridge: MIT Press, 1969), p. 228.

3 Marcum, *The Angolan Revolution,* p. 229.

4 Ibid.

5 Ibid., p. 230. The UPA/FNLA insurgents spoke mostly French, and this limitation made communicating with the local people difficult and proselytising them even more so.

6 Ibid., p. 229.

7 Luís A.M. Grão, *Enfermeiras Pára-quedistas 1961–2002* [Paranurses 1961–2002] (Lisbon: Prefácio, 2006), p. 26.

8 The schools were *Escola de Enfermagem Franciscana Missionárias de Maria* and *Escola de S. Vincente de Paulo*.

9 Luís A.M. Grão, interview by the author, 2 April 1995, Tomar, Portugal.

10 The six "Marias" were: Maria Arminda Pereira, Maria Zulmira Pereira André, Maria do Céu Policarpo, Maria Ivone Reis, Maria de Lurdea Rodrigues, and Maria Nazaré Mascarenhas.

11 Al J. Venter, *Portugal's Guerrilla War: The Campaign for Africa* (Cape Town: John Malherbe, 1973), p. 158.

12 Ibid., p. 160.

13 Luís A.M. Grão, "Os Filhos de Belerofonte" [The Sons of Bellerophon], *Boina Verde*, Supplement (April–June 1993): p. 24.

14 Edgar Pereira da Costa Cardoso, *Presença da Força Aérea em Angola* [Presence of the Air Force in Angola] (Lisbon: Secretaria de Estado de Aeronáutica, 1963), p. 188.

15 Following Hannibal's defeat in 202 B.C., Carthage lay prostrate, and Rome pushed westward from Spain into Lusitania, which proved a difficult venture. A Lusitanian war chief by the name of Viriato or Viriathus, who was originally a simple shepherd, proved more than a match for the Romans and defeated them in battle after battle. Unable to defeat him in combat, in 139 B.C. Rome bribed some of his disloyal followers to murder him as he slept.

16 José Manuel Correia, "Angola, Recordando 1961 e o Início da Actividade da Esquadra 93 "Magnificos" [Angola, Remembering 1961 and the Beginning of Operations of Squadron 93 "The Magnificent Ones"], *Mais Alto* 395 (January–February 2012): p. 21.

17 Manuel Diogo Neto, "Operação da Serra da Canda," personal papers archive, Vol. I, No. Prov. 315, Arquivo Histórico de Força Aérea Portuguesa, Alfragide, p. 4.

18 Costa Cardoso, *Presença da Força Aérea em Angola,* p. 195.

19 Ibid., p. 196.

20 Ibid., p. 196.

21 Inge Brinkman, "Refugees on Routes, Congo/Zaire and the War in Northern Angola (1961–1974)", paper delivered at the international symposium *Angola on the Move: Transport Routes, Communications, and History*, Berlin, 24–26 September 2003, p. 3.

22 Manuel Diogo Neto, "Operação da Serra da Canda", personal papers archive, vol. 1, No. Prov. 315, Arquivo Histórico de Força Aérea Portuguesa, Alfragide, p. 2.

23 Ibid., p. 3.

24 Ibid.

25 Ibid., p. 4.

26 Tomás George Conceição e Silva, "The Portuguese Air Force in the African Wars of 1961–1974" in *Memories of Portugal's African Wars, 1961–1974,* ed. John P. Cann (Quantico: Marine Corps University Foundation, 1998), p. 117.

27 Diogo Neto, "Operação da Serra da Canda", p. 5.

28 Ibid.

29 Costa Cardoso, *Presença da Força Aérea em Angola,* p. 211.

30 Ibid.

31 Luís A.M. Grão, *História das Tropas Pára-Quedistas Portuguesas* [History of the Portuguese Parachute Troops], Volume 2, Angola (Lisbon: Comando das Tropas Aerotransportadas, 1987), pp. 94 and 107.

32 Ibid.

33 John A. Marcum, *The Angolan Revolution,* p. 229.

34 Ibid.

35 Ibid.

36 Ibid., p. 230.

37 Ibid., p. 238. Batista was killed in a 6 February 1962 raid on a Portuguese camp near Bembe when UPA/FNLA forces were surprised in finding unanticipated and prepared Portuguese forces far outnumbering their attackers. Batista's death represented at a minimum a failure of UPA/FNLA intelligence.

38 Costa Cardoso, *Presença da Força Aérea em Angola,* p. 265.

39 Ibid., pp. 266–269.

40 Ibid., p. 269.

41 Ibid., p. 268.

42 Grão, *História das Tropas Pára-Quedistas Portuguesas*, p. 107.

43 Ibid., p. 97.

44 Ibid., p. 99.

45 Ibid., p. 98.

46 Ibid.

47 Ibid., p. 100 and pp. 108–109.

48 Ibid.

49 Arménio Duarte Martins, "Cotova e Falcão" [Skylark and Hawk], *Mais Alto* 311 (February–March 1998): p. 8.

50 Duarte Martins, "Cotova e Falcão," p. 9.

51 Tomás George Conceicão e Silva, interview by the author, 3 April 1995, Lisbon.

52 Duke of Valderano, interview by the author, 17 March 1995, London.

53 Ibid.

54 Brinkman, "War and Identity in Angola", *Lusotopie 2003*: p. 198.

55 John A. Marcum, *The Angolan Revolution, Volume II: Exile Politics and Insurgent Warfare (1962–1976)* (Cambridge: MIT Press, 1978), p. 42.

Chapter 3

1 José de Moura Calheiros, *A Última Missão* [The Last Mission] (Lisbon: Caminhos Romanos, 2010), p. 49.

2 Estado-Maior do Exército, *Resenha Histórico-Militar das Campanhas de África, Vol. III, Dispositivo das Nossas Forças Guiné* [Historical Military Report of the African Campaigns, Vol. III, Disposition of Our Forces in Guiné] (Lisbon: Estado-Maior do Exército, 1989), pp. 20–21.

3 John P. Cann, *Contra-Subversão em África: Como os Portugueses Fizeram a Guerra,1961–1974* [Counter-Subversion in Africa: The Portuguese Way of War, 1961–1974:], 2nd ed., rev. Major General Renato F. Marques Pinto (Lisbon: Prefácio, 2005), p. 25.

4 Ibid.

5 António Afonso and Carlos de Matos Gomes, *Guerra Colonial* [Colonial War] (Lisbon: Notícias, 2001), p. 88.

6 Hélio A. Esteves Felgas, *O Clima do Congo Português* [The Climate of Portuguese Congo] (Carmona: Imprensa Angolana, 1959), p. 9.

7 Estado-Maior do Exército, *Resenha Histórico-Militar das Campanhas de África,* p. 17.

8 José Manuel Correia, "'Rotina' de Guerra: Os F-86F 'Sabre' na Guiné, 2° Parte" ["Route" to War: the F-86F *Sabre* in Guiné], *Mais Alto* 358 (November–December 2005: p. 40.

9 Estado-Maior do Exército, *Resenha Histórico-Militar das Campanhas de África*, p. 27.

10 René Pélissier, *Le Naufrage des Caravelles, Etudes sur la Fin de l□Empire Portugais (1961–1975)* (Orgeval: Editions Pélissier, 1979), p. 208.

11 Alpoim Calvão, "Ataque a Conakry" [Attack on Conakry] in *A Guerra de África 1961–1974* [The African War 1961–1974] (Lisbon: Temas e Debates, 1996), p. 508.

12 Calheiros, *A Última Missão*, p. 58.

13 Ibid.

14 Afonso and Matos Gomes, *Guerra Colonial*, p. 190.

15 Ibid.

16 Calheiros, *A Última Missão*, p. 58.

17 Ibid.

18 José Manuel Correia, "Operação Barracuda: Os Fiat G-91 ao Ataque na Guiné" [Operation Barracuda: The Fiat G-91 on the Attack in Guiné], *Mais Alto* 367 (May–June 2007): p. 23.

19 Ibid., p. 24.

20 Ibid., p. 25.

21 Calheiros, *A Última Missão*, p. 59.

22 Brigadeiro Hélio A. Esteves Felgas, interview by the author, 22 November 1994, Lisbon.

23 General José Manuel de Bethencourt Rodrigues, interview by the author, 9 November 1994, Pedrouços (Lisbon).

24 José Pedro Castanheira, "Ao Serviço de Spínola e Marcelo" [In the service of Spínola and Marcelo], *Expresso* (20 September 1997): p. 56.

25 Ibid.

26 Willem S. van der Waals, *Portugal's War in Angola 1961–1974* (Rivonia: Ashanti, 1993), p. 181.

27 José Pedro Castanheira, "Memórias da Guerra e da Paz: Spínola" [Memories of War and Peace: Spínola], *Expresso Revista* (30 April 1994): p. 78.

28 Douglas L. Wheeler, "The Military and Portuguese Dictatorship, 1926–1974: 'The Honor of the Army,'" in *Contemporary Portugal*, ed. Lawrence S. Graham and Harry M. Makler (Austin: University of Texas Press, 1979), p. 199.

29 Mustafah Dhada, "The Liberation War in Guinea-Bissau Reconsidered," *Journal of Military History* 62 (July 1998): p. 581.

30 Ibid., p. 583.

31 Mustafah Dhada, "Guinea-Bissau's Diplomacy and Liberation Struggle," *Portuguese Studies Review* 4, No. 1 (Spring–Summer 1995): p. 31.

32 Pedro Alexandre Gomes Cardoso, interview by the author, 29 March 1995, Lisbon.

33 Pedro Cardoso, undated personal notes on psychosocial operations in Guiné from 1968 to 1973, pp. 30–31.

34 Patrick Chabal, *Amílcar Cabral: Revolutionarl Leadership and People's War* (Cambridge: Cambridge University Press, 1983), p. 94.

35 Idálio Reis, "Pára-quedistas em Gandembel massacram bigroupo do PAIGC em Set 1968" [Paratroopers in Gandembel destroy a PAIGC bi-group in September 1968], *Luís Graca & Camaradas da Guiné*, 8 July 2007, https://blogueforanadaevaotres.blogspot.com/2007/07/guin-6374-p1930-fotobiografia-da-cca.html (accessed 23 June 2016).

36 Ibid.

37 Ibid.

38 Castanheira, "Ao Serviço de Spínola e Marcelo," p. 28.

39 Calheiros, *A Última Missão*, p. 395.

40 Ibid., p. 396.

41 Ibid., p. 400.

42 António de Spínola, *País sem Rumo: Contributo para a História de uma Revolução* [Country without Direction: Contribution to a History of a Revolution] (Lisbon: Editorial SCIRE, 1978), p. 42.

43 Guilherme Almor de Alpoim Calvão, *De Conakry ao M.D.L.P.* [From Conakry to the M.D.L.P.] (Lisbon: Editorial Intervenção, 1976), pp. 88–96.

44 Castanheira, "Ao Serviço de Spínola e Marcelo," p. 31.

45 Calheiros, *A Última Missão*, pp. 404–405.

46 Ibid., p. 295.

47 Ibid., p. 296.

48 Ibid.

49 Ibid., p. 297.

50 Ibid., p. 299.

51 Ibid., p. 300.

52 Ibid., p. 301.

53 Ibid., pp. 302–303.

54 Ibid., p. 305.

55 Ibid., pp. 322–323.

56 Ibid., p. 325.

57 Ibid., p. 330.

58 Ibid.

59 Ibid., pp. 333–334.

60 Ibid., p. 340.

61 Alexandre Coutinho Lima, *A Retirada da Guileje, 22 Maio 1973: A Verdade dos Factos* [The Withdrawal from Guileje, 22 May 1973: Just the Facts] (Linda-a-Velha: DG edições, 2010), pp. 17–88.

62 Calheiros, *A Última Missão*, p. 513.

63 Ibid.

64 Ibid., p. 516.

65 Ibid., p. 518.

66 Ibid., p. 526.

67 Ibid., p. 536–537.

68 Ibid., p. 533.

69 Ibid., p. 534.

70 Ibid., p. 536.

71 Ibid., p. 539.

72 Ibid., p. 540.

73 Ibid., p. 541.

74 Ibid., p. 544.

Chapter 4

1 Miguel António Gabriel da Silva Machado and António Eleutério Sucena do Carmo, "Tropas Pára-Quedistas Portuguesas" [Portuguese Paratroops], *Boina Verde* 158 (July–September 1991): p. 7.

2 José de Moura Calheiros, *A Última Missão* [The Last Mission] (Porto: Caminhos Romanos, 2010), p. 94.

3 Imigrantes Somos Todas, "Moçambique: A Guerra de Liberação (1964–1974)" [Mozambique: The War of Liberation (1964–1974)]: http://imigrantes.no.sapo.pt/page2mocGLibert.html (accessed 4 February 2010).

4 Fernando E. Ribeiro dos Ramos, "Mozambique: Unfinished Campaign," in *Memories of Portugal's African Wars, 1961–1974*, proceedings of a conference held 10 June 1997, King's College London, ed. John P. Cann (Quantico: Marine Corps University Foundation, 1998), p. 107.

5 Richard Gibson, *African Liberation Movements* (London: Oxford University Press, 1972), p. 281.

6 Malyn Newett, *A History of Mozambique* (London: Hurst & Company, 1995), p. 523.

7 Ibid.

8 Carlos de Matos Gomes, *Moçambique 1970, Operação Nó Górdio* [Mozambique 1970, Operation Gordian Knot] (Lisbon: Prefácio, 2002), p. 13.

9 Ribeiro dos Ramos, "Mozambique: Unfinished Campaign," pp. 107–108.

10 Matos Gomes, *Moçambique 1970*, p. 15.

11 Ibid.

12 Richard Mobley, "The Beira Patrol: Britain's Broken Blockade against Rhodesia," *Naval War College Review* (Winter 2002): p. 65.

13 Ibid., p. 66.

14 Aniceto Afonso and Matos Gomes, *ALCORA: O Acordo Secreto do Colonialismo* [ALCORA: The Secret Accord of Colonialism] (Lisbon: Divina Comédia, 2013), p. 80.

15 J.T.R. Wood, *A matter of weeks rather than months: The Impasse between Harold Wilson and Ian Smith, Sanctions, Aborted Settlements and War, 1965–1969* (Victoria: Tafford, 2008), p. 71.

16 Ibid.

17 Ibid., p. 76.

18 Calheiros, *A Última Missão*, p. 95.

19 Ibid.

20 Ibid.

21 Ibid.

22 Ibid.

23 Ibid.

24 Ibid., p. 96.

25 Ibid.

26 Ibid.

27 Ibid., p. 97.

28 Ibid.

29 Ibid., p. 98.

30 Ibid.

31 Ibid., p. 106.

32 Joaquim Coelho, *O Despertar dos Combatentes* [The Awakening of Combatents] from Espaço Etéreo vivências na guerra colonial: http://www.webkreate.com/espacoetereo/MD9.html (accessed 8 july 2016).

33 Ibid.

34 Calheiros, *A Última Missão,* p. 108.

35 Coelho, *O Despertar dos Combatentes*.

36 Ibid.

37 Calheiros, *A Última Missão*, p. 193.

38 Coelho, *O Despertar dos Combatentes*

39 Calheiros, *A Última Missão,* p. 193.

40 Afonso and Matos Gomes, *ALCORA*, p. 155.

41 Matos Gomes, *Moçambique 1970,* p. 6.

42 Ibid.

43 Alfredo Cruz, *O Voo do Falcão: Piloto de Combate, Moçambique* [Flight of the Falcon: Combat Pilot, Mozambique] (Lisbon: Fronteira do Caos, 2014), 58–59.

44 Ibid., p. 212.

45 Matos Gomes, *Moçambique 1970,* p. 65.

46 Ibid., p. 10.

47 Ibid., p. 28.

48 Ibid.

49 Ibid.

50 Ibid., p. 61.

51 Ibid., p. 65.

52 Ibid.

53 Malyn Newitt, *A History of Mozambique*, pp. 531–532.

54 Adelino Serras Pires and Fiona Claire Capstick, *The Winds of Havoc* (New York: St. Martin□s Press, 2001), p. 83.

55 Al J. Venter, *The Zambesi Salient* (Capetown: Howard Timmins, 1974), pp. 47–48.

56 Henrik Ellert, *The Rhodesian Front War, Counter-insurgency and Guerrilla Warfare 1962–1980* (Gweru, Zimbabwe: Mambo Press, 1993), p. 88.

Chapter 5

1 António Lopes Pires Nunes, *Angola 1966–74, Vitória Militar no Leste* [Angola 1966–74, Military Victory in the East] (Lisbon: Prefácio, 2002), p. 10.

2 António Lopes Pires Nunes, *Siroco: Os Comandos no Leste de Angola* [Siroco: The Commandos in the East of Angola] (Lisbon: Associação de Comandos, 2013), p. 45.

3 Comissão para o Estudo das Campanhas de África (1961–1974), *Resenha Histórico-Militar das Campanhas de África (1961–1974), 2° Volume, Dispositivo das Nossas Forças, Angola* [Historical-Military Report of the African Campaigns (1961–1974), 2° Volume, Disposition of Our Forces, Angola] (Lisbon, Estado-Maior do Exército, 1989), p. 127.

4 Pires Nunes, *Angola 1966–74, Vitória Militar no Leste,* p. 40.

5 Ibid.

6 Comissão para o Estudo das Campanhas de África, *Resenha Histórico-Militar das Campanhas de África 1961–1974, 6 Volume, Aspectos da Actividade Operacional, Tomo I, Angola–Livro 2* [Historical Military Report on the African Campaigns 1961–1974, 6 Volume, Aspects of Operational Activity, Tome I, Angola, Book 2] (Lisbon: Estado-Maior de Exército, 2006), p. 353.

7 Ibid.

8 Ibid., pp. 223–228.

9 Ibid.

10 Adelino Gomes, "Exército e UNITA Colaboraram antes de 74" [Army and UNITA Collaborate before 74], *Público* (19 December 1995), pp. 2-4; and Óscar Cardoso, "Criador dos Flechas" [Creator of the Flechas] in José Freire Antunes, *A Guerra de África, 1961–1974, Volume 1* [The War in Africa, 1961–1974, Volume 1] (Lisbon: Temas e Debates, 1996), pp. 409–410.

11 Dalila Cabrita Mateus, *A PIDE/DGS na Guerra Colonial 1961–1974* [The PIDE/DGS in the Colonial War 1961–1974] (Lisbon: Terramar, 2004), pp. 199–207.

12 Pires Nunes, *Angola 1966–74, Vitória Militar no Leste,* p. 19.

13 Ibid., p. 42.

14 Pires Nunes, *Siroco*, p. 89. An exarch is the viceroy of a Byzantine emperor.

15 Ibid.

16 Ibid. Américo Boavida, was an Angolan physician also known as *N'Gola Kimbanda* or "chief healer," who attended Liceu Salvador Correia in Luanda and then travelled to Portugal to study medicine at the University of Porto. He returned to Angola in 1955 and entered private practice specialising in obstetrics and gynaecology until 1960, when he joined the MPLA. He became a member of the MPLA Directing Committee for external relations, based in Léopoldville, where he also led the Angolan Volunteer Corps for Refugee Assistance (CVAAR) from 1962 to 1963. In 1963, he left the Congo after CVAAR was banned by the Congolese government and worked in Rabat for three years. It was in Morocco that he wrote *Angola: Five Centuries of Portuguese Exploitation*, an important Marxist critique of colonial rule. In June 1967, he returned to the fight and practiced and taught a mixture of modern and traditional medicine to members of the insurgent army. Following his death in 1968 and Angolan independence in 1975, a hospital in Luanda was named for him.

17 Ibid.

18 Ibid., p. 90.

19 Ibid.

20 Ibid., p. 91.

21 Joaquim M. Mensurado, *Os Páras na Guerra, 1961–63 and 1968–72* [Paras at War, 1961–63 and 1968–72] (Lisbon: Prefácio, 2002), pp. 52–53.

22 Ibid., pp. 54–55.

23 Ibid., p. 55.

24 Ibid., p. 56.

25 Carlos Acabado, *Kinda e Outras Histórias de uma Guerra Esquecida* [Kinda and Other Stories of a Forgotten War] (Linda-a-Velha: DG Edições, 2011), pp. 154–155.

26 Hélio Felgas, "Opinião" [Opinion], as quoted in *Resenha Histórico-Militar das Campanhas de África, 1961–1974, 6th Volume, Tome I, Book 2, Angola* by Comissião para o Estudo das Campanhas de África (1961–1974) (Lisbon: Estado-Maior do Exército, 2006), p. 450.

27 António Silva Cardoso, *Angola: Anatomia de uma Tragédia* [Angola: Anatomy of a Tragedy] (Lisbon: Oficina de Livro, 2000), p. 302.

28 Ibid., p. 292.

Chapter 6

1 The International Police for the Defence of the State (*Polícia Internacional e de Defesa do Estado* or PIDE) was given a less tainted name in 1969 by Marcelo Caetano, the new prime minister, as the Directorate-General of Security (*Direcção Geral de Segurança* or DGS). DGS operations in the *ultramar* were aimed at intelligence gathering, and this was done through agents in Zaire, Zambia, and Tanzania, the questioning of enemy prisoners, and operations of the *flechas* within Angola and later in Mozambique and Guiné. For a fuller treatment of *flecha* operations please see John P. Cann, *The Flechas: Insurgent Hunting in Eastern Angola, 1965–1974* (Solihull: Helion, 2013).

2 Direcção Geral de Segurança, Acções das Nossas Forces [Actions of Our Forces], DGS-Angola, 22 June 1973, SDGN 1802, Intelligence Report 677, Arquivo da Defesa Nacional, Paço do Arcos, Portugal.

3 Ricardo dos Santos Cubas, Geraldo Estevens, Guilherme Costa Santos, and José Augusto Barrigas Queiroga, "Ensinamentos da Guerra em Angola" [Teachings of the War in Angola], proceedings of a conference "Almoços da AFAP," January 2011, p. 7.

4 Ibid.

5 Ibid., p. 9.

6 Ibid., p. 10.

7 Ibid.

8 Ibid.

9 Ibid.

10 Ibid., p. 8.

11 Ibid., p. 11.

12 Ibid.

13 Ibid.

14 Ibid., p. 12.

15 Ibid.

16 Ibid., p. 13.

17 Ibid., pp. 13–14.

18 Ibid., p. 14.

19 Ibid.

20 Ibid., pp. 15–16.

21 Ibid., p. 16.

22 Ibid.

23 Ibid.

24 Ibid., p. 17.

25 Ibid., p. 18.

26 Ibid.

27 Ibid., p. 19.

28 Ibid.

29 Ibid.

30 Ibid., p. 20.

31 Ibid.

32 Direcção Geral de Segurança, Acções das Nossas Forces [Actions of Our Forces], DGS-Angola, 10 July 1973, SDGN 1802, Intelligence Report 754, Arquivo da Defesa Nacional, Paço do Arcos, Portugal.

33 Ibid.

34 Tomás Francisco Ferreira was a commander in the MPLA areas in the north of Angola along the Congo frontier in 1961.

35 Direcção Geral de Segurança, Acções das Nossas Forces [Actions of Our Forces], DGS-Angola, 18 July 1973, SDGN 1802, Intelligence Report 766, Arquivo da Defesa Nacional, Paço do Arcos, Portugal.

BIBLIOGRAPHY

Afonso, Aniceto, and Carlos de Matos Gomes. *Guerra Colonial.* [Colonial War]. Lisbon: Notícias, 2000.

Antunes, José Freire. *A Guerra de África 1961–1974.* [The War of Africa 1961–1974]. Lisbon: Temas e Debates, 1996.

Chamberlain, Ernest. *Forgotten Men: Timorese in Special Operations during World War II.* Point Lonsdale: Privately printed, 2010.

Cleary, Paul. *The Men Who Came Out of the Ground: A Gripping Account of Australia's First Commando Campaign, Timor, 1942.* Sydney: Hachette Australia, 2010.

Martinho Grão, Luís António. *Enfermeiras Pára-quedistas 1961–2002.* [Paranurses 1961–2002]. Lisbon: Prefácio, 2006.

_____. *História das Tropas Pára-Quedistas Portuguesas, Volume I, Tancos 1955–1961.* [History of the Portuguese Paratroops, Volume I, Tancos 1955–1961]. Lisbon: Comando das Tropas Aerotransportadas, 1987.

Matos Gomes, Carlos de. *Moçambique 1970, Operação Nó Górdio.* [Mozambique 1970, Operation Gordian Knot]. Lisbon: Prefácio, 2002.

Mensurado, Joaquim M. *Os Páras na Guerra, 1961–63 and 1968–72.* [Paras at War, 1961–63 and 1968–72]. Lisbon: Prefácio, 2002.

Moura Calheiros, José de. *A Última Missão.* [The Last Missio]. Lisbon: Caminhos Romanos, 2010.

Pires Nunes, António Lopes. *Siroco: Os Comandos no Leste de Angola.* [Siroco: The Commandos in the East of Angola]. Lisbon: Associação de Comandos, 2013.

_____. *Angola 1966–1974, Vitória Militar no Leste.* [Angola 1966–1974, Military Victory in the East]. Lisbon: Prefácio, 2002.

Silva Machado, Miguel António Gabriel da, and António Eleutério Sucena do Carmo. "Tropas Pára-Quedistas Portuguesas." [Portuguese Paratroops]. *Boina Verde* 158 (July–September 1991).

Van der Waals, Willem S. *Portugal□s War in Angola 1961–1974.* Rivonia: Ashanti Publishing, 1993.

Venter, Al J. *The Zambesi Salient: Conflict in Southern Africa.* Cape Town: Howard Timmins, 1974.

_____. *Portugal's Insurgent War, The Campaign for Africa.* Cape Town: John Malherbe, 1973.

ACKNOWLEDGMENTS

I wish to thank General Tomás George Conceição Silva and General Jorge Manuel Brochado de Miranda for their skilful guidance and support in the research and writing of this book. General Conceição Silva furnished many of the photographs from his extensive personal collection, and for that I am most appreciative. General Brochado de Miranda expertly guided my research, and both have been perfect advisors and friends throughout.

I am most grateful for the interviews granted to me by General Kaúlza de Arriaga almost twenty years ago and our conversations and correspondence on the formation of the Portuguese Air Force and the Paras. Likewise I am indebted to Brigadier José Agostinho Melo Ferreira Pinto, who also many years ago talked to me about the Paras in Africa. My deep appreciation likewise goes to Colonel A. Marques de Carvalho, who introduced me to the important role of the Paras in counterinsurgency and made me a gift of the first volume of the *History of the Portuguese Paratroopers*. I am also deeply grateful for the several hours that Colonel Luís A. Martinho Grão spent with me at his home in Tomar many years ago talking about the Paras and the innovative Para-nurses. *Comandante* Abel Melo e Sousa took many photographs while in the Cantanhez Peninsula of Guiné during the war and shared his work with me, for which I am most grateful. I am likewise indebted to Dr. José Manuel Correia and Lieutenant Colonel (pilot aviator) João José Brandão Ferreira, both good friends who generously spent many hours explaining the details of operations in Africa.

Finally, I owe a particular debt to my wife Anne, who lived patiently with the domestic chaos of this work.

ABOUT THE AUTHOR

John P. Cann is a Research Fellow and retired Professor of National Security Studies at Marine Corps University, a former member of the research staff at the Institute for Defense Analyses, and former Scholar-in-Residence at the University of Virginia. He earned his doctorate in War Studies at King's College London in 1996, published *Counterinsurgency in Africa* in 1997, *Memories of Portugal's African Wars, 1961–1975* (ed.) in 1998, *The Brown Waters of Africa* in 2008, The Flechas in 2013, Flight Plan Africa in 2015, and some thirty plus articles on small wars over the years. He is a retired naval captain and flight officer specializing in open ocean reconnaissance aviation and served in a variety of aviation assignments, including command. He has been awarded the Portuguese Navy Cross Medal and the Medal of Dom Afonso Henriques for his writings on conflict in Lusophone Africa. He is an Associate Member of the Academia de Marinha.